Fun in the Sun with
JUMBLE
BrainBusters™

The Ultimate in Sizzling Puzzle Fun!

David L. Hoyt and Russell L. Hoyt

TRIUMPH
BOOKS
CHICAGO

This book is available in quantity at special discounts
for your group or organization.

For further information, contact:

Triumph Books
814 North Franklin Street
Chicago, Illinois 60610
(312) 939-3330

Printed in the United States of America

ISBN 978-1-57243-733-3

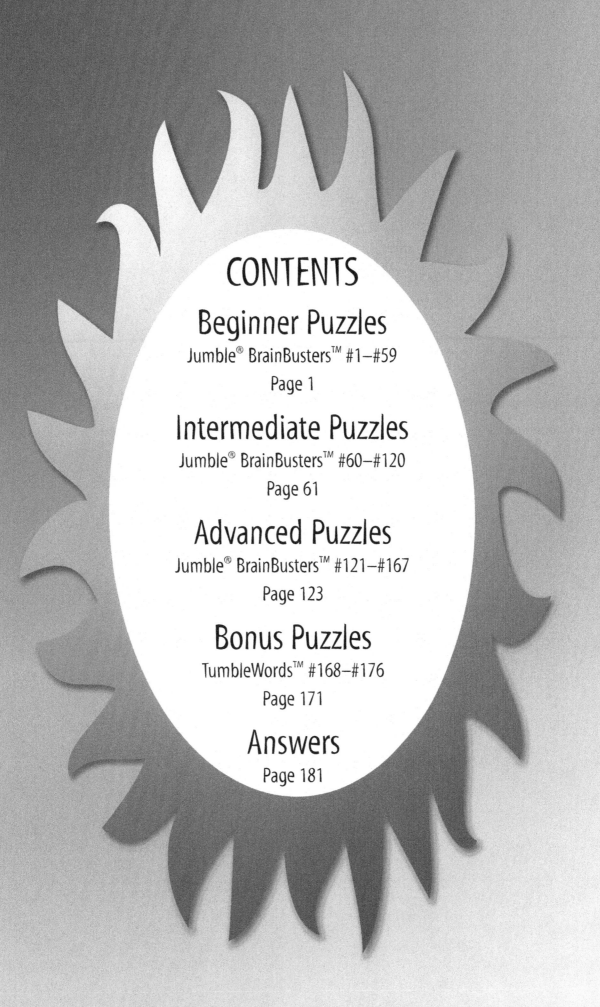

CONTENTS

Beginner Puzzles

JUMBLE®

BrainBusters™

Beginner Puzzles

BASEBALL

JUMBLE BrainBusters™

Unscramble the Jumbles, one letter to each square, to spell words related to baseball.

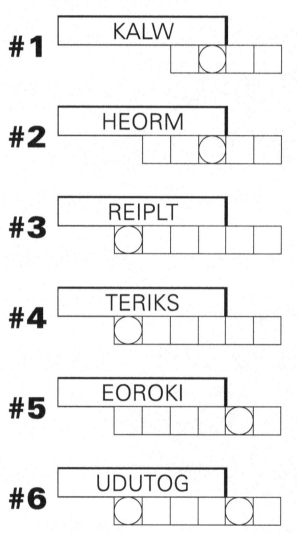

#1 KALW

#2 HEORM

#3 REIPLT

#4 TERIKS

#5 EOROKI

#6 UDUTOG

Arrange the circled letters to solve the mystery answer.

Interesting Baseball Facts

Barry Bonds hit 73 home runs during the 2001 baseball season.

The New York Yankees were the first team to travel to a game via airplane.

An official baseball has 150 yards of wool yarn inside it.

MYSTERY ANSWER

THE NAME GAME

Unscramble the Jumbles, one letter to each square, to spell last names, as suggested by the first name clues.

Walter _____, born in 1928

#1 DEMOLNA

Maria _____, born in 1955

#6 RESIVRH

Jane _____, born in 1950

#2 ELPAYU

Tommy _____, born in 1951

#7 GFEHIRIL

Julia _____, born in 1967

#3 RTREOSB

Nancy _____, born in 1921

#8 GNRAAE

John _____, born in 1942

#4 CFAHRTSO

Peter _____, born in 1938

#9 NGJIENSN

David _____, born in 1950

#5 SDCSIYA

Donald _____, born in 1946

#10 MPRUT

BIRDS

Unscramble the Jumbles, one letter to each square, to spell varieties of birds.

#1 EODV

#2 CWOR

#3 RNEVA

#4 GIPENO

#5 NKHCIEC

#6 VRLUETU

Arrange the circled letters to solve the mystery answer.

Box of Clues

Stumped? Maybe you can find a clue below.

-Domesticated farm bird
-Glossy, black passerine bird
-Mourning _____
-Widespread dove relative
-Stout-bodied game bird
-Large raptorial bird
-Glossy, black corvine bird

MYSTERY ANSWER

STARTS WITH AND ENDS WITH A VOWEL

Unscramble the Jumbles, one letter to each square, to spell words that start with and end with a vowel.

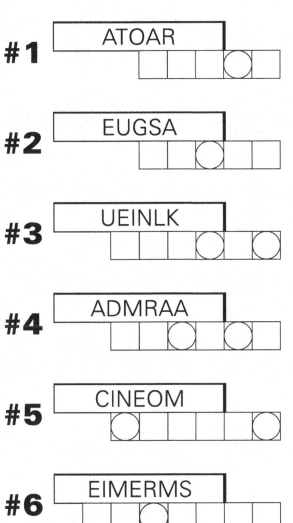

#1 ATOAR

#2 EUGSA

#3 UEINLK

#4 ADMRAA

#5 CINEOM

#6 EIMERMS

Arrange the circled letters to solve the mystery answer.

Box of Clues

Stumped? Maybe you can find a clue below.

-Fleet
-Arterial trunk
-Utilization, employment
-Plunge into something
-Different than
-_____ tax
-Current, instant

MYSTERY ANSWER

JUMBLE TRIVIA

Unscramble the Jumbles, one letter
to each square, to spell words as
suggested by the trivia clues.

#1 This country is about 265 miles wide and 2,880 miles long.

CLEIH

#2 Brontology is the study of this.

EDTNRUH

#3 Until 2000, the sucre was the official currency unit of _____.

ODURACE

#4 This state was named after a valley in Pennsylvania.

GIYWONM

#5 This U.S. president was the first president inaugurated in Washington, D.C.

OFREFJNES

Arrange the circled letters to solve the mystery answer.

This type of dog was bred and raised by the aristocracy. In fact, for approximately 700 years it was illegal under English law for a commoner to own one.

MYSTERY ANSWER

LAVERNE & SHIRLEY

JUMBLE BrainBusters™

Unscramble the Jumbles, one letter to each square, to spell words related to the television show *Laverne & Shirley*.

#1 NLYEN

#2 TSOZH

#3 MCSOIT

#4 CMIAENR

#5 SALRLMHA

#6 KEWMIUEAL

LAVERNE & SHIRLEY

Box of Clues

Stumped? Maybe you can find a clue below.

-Actress who played Laverne
-_____ Kosnowski
-*Laverne & Shirley* setting
-Eddie Mekka role
-What Laverne and Shirley were
-Type of show
-Name of the brewery where Laverne and Shirley worked

Arrange the circled letters to solve the mystery answer.

MYSTERY ANSWER

WEATHER

Unscramble the Jumbles, one letter
to each square, to spell words related
to weather.

#1 AHIL
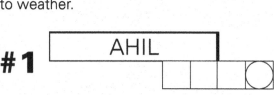

#2 NOFTR

#3 OMRST

#4 RDEGESE

#5 AFRANLIL

#6 ASFRCOTE

Box of Clues

Stumped? Maybe you can find a clue
below.

-Warm or cold _____
-Temperature units
-Weather disturbance
-A reason to head for higher
 ground
-Ice pellets
-Amount of liquid precipitation
-Prediction

Arrange the circled letters
to solve the mystery answer.

MYSTERY ANSWER

FIND THE JUMBLES

Unscramble the Jumbles, one letter
to each square, to spell words.

#1 RIVYO

#2 ABLKC

#3 MEAVU

#4 NBRWO

#5 LVOEIT

#6 PLUPER

#7 EWLYLO

#8 DLAVEERN

Find and circle the answers (from above) in the grid of letters below.

```
P R O U N P U N C E Z X E R W P
U U T L J U U U B I Y N B P I O
H T I E B W C R R O P E R X N L
G B U K O B R E P V C O O I T N
H P L L P Y L E O L O P W O E P
Y A L A R R V U L K E I N R L O
G E P O C U U P O J P P U K O L
Y F V R A K R E X N N L P O I U
G I K M L A V E N D E R P L V P
```

WARS AND THE MILITARY

Unscramble the Jumbles, one letter to each square, to spell words related to wars and the military.

#1 GIESE

#2 LUTBEL

#3 POWANE

#4 MBORBE

#5 FGRUIEN

#6 CDTREOFE

Box of Clues

Stumped? Maybe you can find a clue below.

-Side-changer
-Persistent or serious attack
-Small missile
-A means of contending against another
-Type of military organization
-A reason to take cover
-Type of airplane

Arrange the circled letters to solve the mystery answer.

MYSTERY ANSWER

ADJECTIVES

Unscramble the Jumbles, one letter to each square, to spell adjectives.

#1 UDCLI

#2 ABVRE

#3 ASHYT

#4 KBALE

#5 LCOLA

#6 OGLYSS

#7 PRUGMY

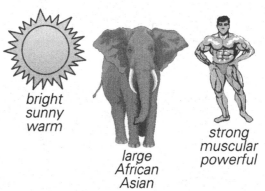

*bright
sunny
warm*

*large
African
Asian*

*strong
muscular
powerful*

Box of Clues

Stumped? Maybe you can find a clue below.

- -Irritable
- -Suffused with light
- -Shiny, slick
- -Ghastly
- -Courageous
- -Made in a hurry
- -Depressing, grim
- -Nearby

Arrange the circled letters to solve the mystery answer.

MYSTERY ANSWER

JUMBLE RIDDLES

Unscramble the mixed up letters to
reveal the punch lines to the riddles.

#1 What is a ghoul's favorite
food?

AGOSULH

#2 What famous Greek might
have invented baseball?

MEHOR

#3 What can stay hot in the
refrigerator?

ARMSTDU

#4 What travels around the
world but stays in a
corner?

TASAPM

#5 Where can you find cards
on a ship?

TONHKEDEC

#6 If fish lived on land, where
would they live?

NIFNLIADN

ABBREVIATIONS

JUMBLE
BrainBusters™

Unscramble the Jumbles, one letter
to each square, to spell words that are
often abbreviated.

#1 UENOC

#2 KTIETC

#3 DOPUNS

#4 UMNEBR

#5 EFERERE

#6 BEDMCERE

Sec.
Frwy.
Dup.
Ave.
Feb.
Ref.
Diam.
Dist.
Dec.
Aug.
Bldg.
No.
Oct.
Sept.
Blvd.
Lbs.
Tkt.
Eve.
Sun.
Capt.
Oz.

Arrange the circled letters
to solve the mystery answer.

MYSTERY ANSWER

13

STARTS WITH B

Unscramble the Jumbles, one letter to each square, to spell words that start with *B*.

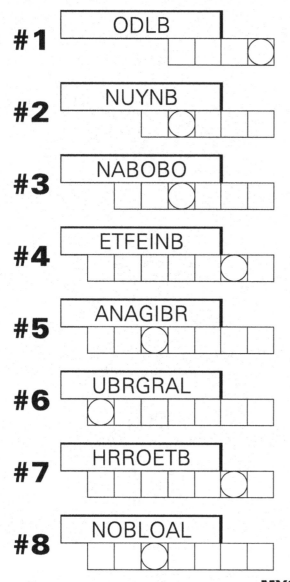

#1 ODLB

#2 NUYNB

#3 NABOBO

#4 ETFEINB

#5 ANAGIBR

#6 UBRGRAL

#7 HRROETB

#8 NOBLOAL

Arrange the circled letters to solve the mystery answer.

Box of Clues

Stumped? Maybe you can find a clue below.

- Something that promotes well-being
- A word that can apply to a man or a boy
- _____ alarm
- Rabbit
- Good deal
- Brave
- Type of songbird
- Bag of lighter-than-air material
- Type of primate

MYSTERY ANSWER

POETRY

JUMBLE
BrainBusters™

Unscramble the Jumbles, one letter
to each square, to spell words found
in the poem.

#1 MHKOACM

#2 ZEEBER

#3 ERCREEFA

#4 NCAED

#5 RILENCHD

#6 FRDIT

#7 EIDLA

LEISURE TIME
by Kim Nolan

A big comfy _____ #1
The shade from some trees
A perfect blue sky
A delicate _____ #2

A good book to read
An ice-cold pitcher of tea
No obligations in sight
Just completely _____ #3

Clouds _____ #4 overhead
The sound of _____ #5 at play
You _____ #6 off to sleep
An _____ #7 summer day

Arrange the circled letters
to solve the mystery answer.
(The mystery answer is not
in the poem.)

MYSTERY ANSWER

15

puzzle 15

JUMBLE® CONNECTIONS

JUMBLE
BrainBusters™

Unscramble the Jumbles, one letter to each square, to spell words that fit into the puzzle below.

ACROSS
- **#1** USNBUNR
- **#5** EGLOBN
- **#7** NOUDM
- **#8** SEIRHES
- **#10** AHSR
- **#12** SMKITAE
- **#13** LSOGNA

DOWN
- **#1** RUMSME
- **#2** HRABNC
- **#3** GUDEN
- **#4** SLACS
- **#5** YBRER
- **#6** AGELZLE
- **#8** HPBCUA
- **#9** FSARIA
- **#11** SMIAS

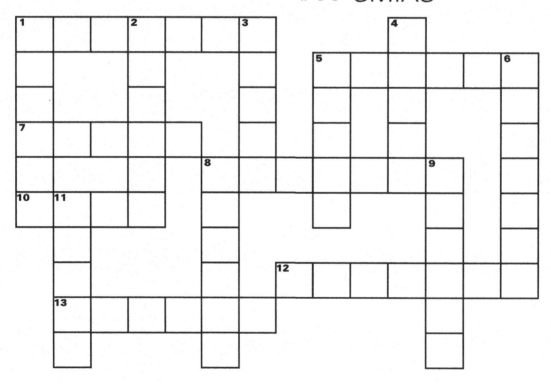

16

U.S. STATES

Unscramble the Jumbles, one letter to each square, to spell names of U.S. states.

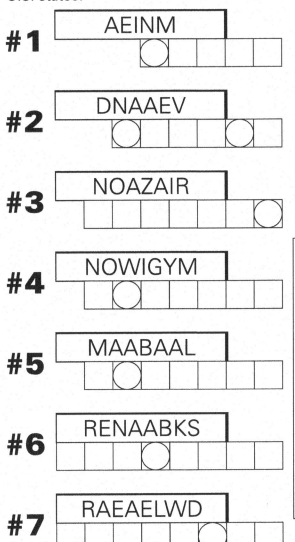

#1 AEINM

#2 DNAAEV

#3 NOAZAIR

#4 NOWIGYM

#5 MAABAAL

#6 RENAABKS

#7 RAEAELWD

Arrange the circled letters to solve the mystery answer.

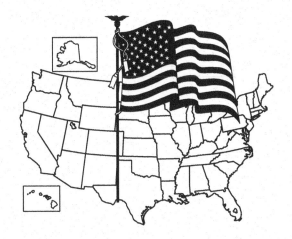

Interesting U.S. State Facts

New Mexico's official state bird is the roadrunner.

The smallest U.S. state in area west of the Mississippi River is Hawaii.

The state of Oregon has a city named Sisters and another city called Brothers.

MYSTERY ANSWER

PLANET EARTH

JUMBLE
BrainBusters™

Unscramble the Jumbles, one letter
to each square, to spell words related
to planet Earth.

#1 HLIL

#2 EKRCE

#3 AILSDN

#4 LVLYEA

#5 ULNEGJ

#6 NRDUAT

Box of Clues

Stumped? Maybe you can find a clue
below. (No clue for the mystery answer.)

-Natural depression
-Treeless plain
-Natural elevation
-Stream
-Tropical forest
-Tract of land surrounded by
 water

Arrange the circled letters
to solve the mystery answer.

MYSTERY ANSWER

JUMBLE® TRIVIA

JUMBLE®
BrainBusters™

Unscramble the Jumbles, one letter to each square, to spell words as suggested by the trivia clues.

#1 This U.S. president fathered 15 children.

ETLRY

#2 This space station was launched into orbit in 1973.

ASYLBK

#3 No settlement in New _____ is more than 75 miles from the sea.

NELDAZA

#4 _____ is about the same size as Maine.

ANSTLDOC

#5 This secure area takes up 110,000 acres.

TFOXKORN

Arrange the circled letters to solve the mystery answer.

The _____ Bridge was completed in 1883.

MYSTERY ANSWER

STARTS AND ENDS WITH THE SAME LETTER

JUMBLE BrainBusters™

Unscramble the Jumbles, one letter to each square, to spell words that start and end with the same letter.

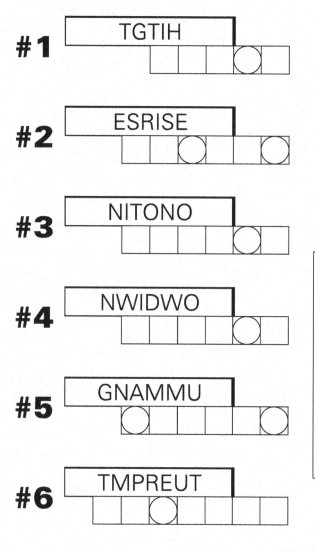

#1 TGTIH

#2 ESRISE

#3 NITONO

#4 NWIDWO

#5 GNAMMU

#6 TMPREUT

RADAR
ARENA POP GOING
RIVER HIGH
DICED CRYPTIC

Box of Clues

Stumped? Maybe you can find a clue below.

-A musical instrument
-Snug
-World _____
-Idea
-_____ cloud
-Picture _____
-Tall TV detective

Arrange the circled letters to solve the mystery answer.

MYSTERY ANSWER

RHYMES WITH . . .

Unscramble the Jumbles, one letter to each square, to spell words that will each have a corresponding rhyming clue.

JUMBLE BrainBusters™

GO · · · NO
TON · · · FUN
BACK · · · STACK
STUCK · · · TRUCK
MISTER · · · SISTER
SCANDAL · · · SANDAL

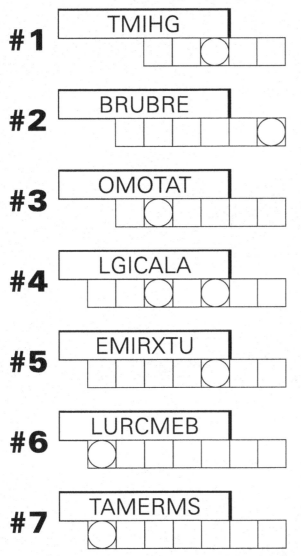

#1 TMIHG

#2 BRUBRE

#3 OMOTAT

#4 LGICALA

#5 EMIRXTU

#6 LURCMEB

#7 TAMERMS

Box of Clues

Stumped? Maybe you can find a clue below.

-Rhymes with *facial*
-Rhymes with *slight*
-Rhymes with *potato*
-Rhymes with *hammer*
-Rhymes with *spacious*
-Rhymes with *blubber*
-Rhymes with *fixture*
-Rhymes with *rumble*

Arrange the circled letters to solve the mystery answer.

MYSTERY ANSWER

MATH

Unscramble the Jumbles, one letter to each square, so that each equation is correct.

For example:

NONTEOEOW

O N E + O N E = T W O

#1 ZONEOEEONR

⬭□□ − ⬭□□ = □□□⬭

#2 WOFRTWUOOT

□□⬭⬭ − □□□ = □⬭□

#3 ETFVIEEINVF

□□□□□ + ⬭□□□□ = ⬭□□□

#4 TSISXLEIVWXE

□□□□ + □□□□ = ⬭⬭□□□□

Then arrange the circled letters to solve the mystery equation.

MYSTERY EQUATION

⬭⬭⬭ × ⬭⬭⬭ = ⬭⬭⬭⬭

ANIMALS

JUMBLE
BrainBusters™

Unscramble the Jumbles, one letter to each square, to spell names of animals.

#1 OFGR

#2 ALCEM

#3 RZDLIA

#4 AIBRTB

Box of Clues

Stumped? Maybe you can find a clue below. (No clue for the mystery answer.)

-Angora _____
-Tree ____
-Desert mammal
-Powerful cat
-Spider _____
-Type of reptile

#5 ACORGU

#6 EOMYKN

Arrange the circled letters to solve the mystery answer.

MYSTERY ANSWER

FIND THE JUMBLES®

Unscramble the Jumbles, one letter to each square, to spell words.

#1 ANWP

#2 EMVO

#3 EPCEI

#4 HECKC

#5 RBODA

#6 TMHCA

#7 GKITNH

#8 SBIHPO

Find and circle the answers (from above) in the grid of letters below.

```
C A F H I N J K P L H N I O P J
R X P R W I S O K T X C B B N A
B F C A L H H K G E O D A O L C
N S P K L S H X L N M U I A B G
J C T B I L F U E W E A J R F H
M I V B H F R C H E C K T D G I
H O R X E G E S E S D F P C I K
G C V H L I B G J I O P U L H L
D S N E P V N K N I G H T P O F
```

MATH

JUMBLE
BrainBusters™

Unscramble the Jumbles,
one letter to each square, so
that each equation is correct.

For example:

NONTEOEOW
ONE + ONE = TWO

#1

NOENOEENO

☐ ☐ ⊙ × ☐ ⊙ ☐ = ☐ ⊙ ☐

#2

NSVEEFVTOIEW

☐ ☐ ☐ ⊙ ☐ − ☐ ⊙ ☐ ☐ = ⊙ ☐ ☐

#3

GREOFUOITHTW

☐ ⊙ ☐ ☐ × ☐ ☐ ☐ = ☐ ⊙ ☐ ⊙ ☐

#4

REFOTREOEHNU

☐ ☐ ☐ ☐ − ☐ ☐ ☐ ☐ ⊙ = ☐ ⊙ ☐

Then arrange the
circled letters to solve
the mystery equation.

MYSTERY EQUATION

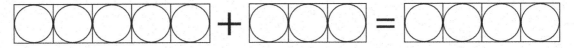

○○○○○ + ○○○ = ○○○○

25

JUMBLE® CONNECTIONS

Unscramble the Jumbles, one letter to each square, to spell words that fit into the puzzle below.

ACROSS

- #1 TISPDUE
- #5 HTWTAR
- #7 EUSRH
- #8 CDEIELB
- #10 VENE
- #12 TABHIAT
- #13 UDUSEN

DOWN

- #1 XLDEUE
- #2 EIGONP
- #3 UNESE
- #4 AEARW
- #5 TPUIL
- #6 TRNMOET
- #8 DTOKEC
- #9 RETLTE
- #11 UALVE

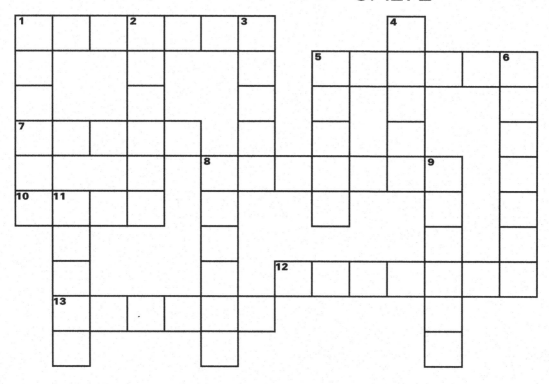

JUMBLE® RIDDLES

Unscramble the mixed up letters to reveal the punch lines to the riddles.

#1 When it rains cats and dogs, what do you step into?

PSODLEO

#2 What is a rifle with three barrels?

TERIAFL

#3 Where do sick steamships go?

DTOOECHKT

#4 What kind of ribbon do politicians use?

EDETAPR

#5 How do undertakers speak?

RAVYGEL

#6 What grows larger the more you take away?

LAHEO

JUMBLE® TRIVIA

Unscramble the Jumbles, one letter to each square, to spell words as suggested by the trivia clues.

#1 This U.S. state's nickname is the "Pine Tree State."

NMIEA

#2 _____ has an equatorial diameter of about 30,700 miles, nearly four times that of Earth.

TENNEPU

#3 Like the camel, this animal can go without water for long periods of time.

RGFIFEA

#4 There are about 2,000 species of _____.

STIRMEET

#5 Terry _____ was the #1 NFL draft choice in 1970.

SHABWARD

Arrange the circled letters to solve the mystery answer.

This creature can flap its wings 50 to 75 beats per second.

MYSTERY ANSWER

FIND THE JUMBLES

Unscramble the Jumbles, one letter to each square, to spell words.

#1 DPUNO

#2 UNOEC

#3 RBRLEA

#4 UBESHL

#5 AGLONL

#6 CNMRIO

#7 FUGLORN

#8 OPTESOAN

Find and circle the answers (from above) in the grid of letters below.

```
A C H Z C D Z E D G H Z O P U Z
N F P J P N I N R R P I P G G K
O B H A O O U N C E I O N A N L
O C S F R O P F T Z L R H L O I
P O N P P J H V E U G B E L L T
S M I C R O N O R U P H U O R E
A C S D E H K N L J S N O N U J
E W B A R R E L P U Z Y S R F P
T R E R R Z B H B H K R V X U T
```

ADJECTIVES

JUMBLE BrainBusters™

Unscramble the Jumbles, one letter
to each square, to spell adjectives.

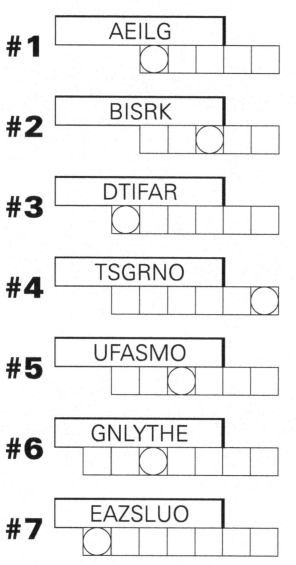

#1 AEILG

#2 BISRK

#3 DTIFAR

#4 TSGRNO

#5 UFASMO

#6 GNLYTHE

#7 EAZSLUO

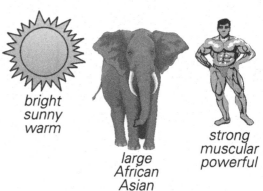

*bright
sunny
warm*

*large
African
Asian*

*strong
muscular
powerful*

Box of Clues

Stumped? Maybe you can find a clue
below.

-Floating, free from restraint
-Of considerable duration
-Lively, invigorating
-Marvelous
-Enthusiastic
-Prominent
-Muscular
-Moving with ease and grace

Arrange the circled letters
to solve the mystery answer.

MYSTERY ANSWER

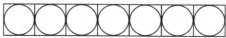

JUMBLE® CONNECTIONS

JUMBLE. BrainBusters™

Unscramble the Jumbles, one letter to each square, to spell words that fit into the puzzle below.

ACROSS

- **#1** GSOGLGE
- **#5** XTOETR
- **#7** UBSCA
- **#8** PRHPEAS
- **#10** UTNP
- **#12** RCOSOTE
- **#13** NAORDW

DOWN

- **#1** GPOSIS
- **#2** MGAITB
- **#3** YSTEL
- **#4** SMUPT
- **#5** GTHIE
- **#6** WSTRITE
- **#8** SPARYT
- **#9** YRENTS
- **#11** NUINO

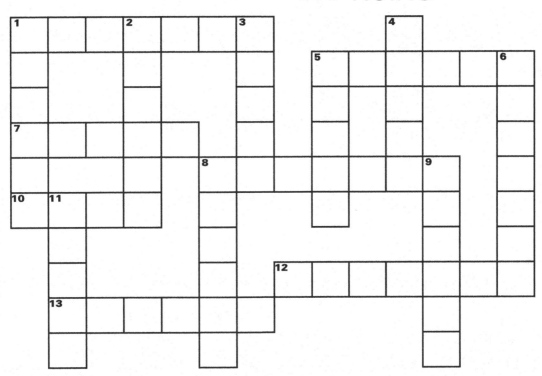

STARTS AND ENDS WITH THE SAME LETTER

Unscramble the Jumbles, one letter to each square, to spell words that start and end with the same letter.

JUMBLE BrainBusters™

RADAR
ARENA POP GOING
RIVER HIGH
DICED CRYPTIC

#1 OELEP

#2 UYMYM

#3 TSATSU

#4 PCIRYTC

#5 CDISRDA

#6 ROEOSTR

Box of Clues

Stumped? Maybe you can find a clue below.

-Mysterious
-Type of bird
-Subdue
-Delectable
-Chuck
-Slip away, escape
-_____ report

Arrange the circled letters to solve the mystery answer.

MYSTERY ANSWER

JUMBLE RIDDLES

Unscramble the mixed up letters to
reveal the punch lines to the riddles.

#1 What is easy to get into
but hard to get out of?

LUTRBEO

#2 What doesn't exist but has
a name?

ONHNTIG

#3 What has a big mouth but
can't talk?

RVARIE

#4 What flies when it's on and
floats when it's off?

EFARTHAE

#5 What is a foreign ant?

NIARPTOTM

#6 What gets harder to catch
the faster you run?

OYURREHBAT

BASEBALL TEAMS

Unscramble the Jumbles, one letter to each square, to spell names of Major League baseball teams.

#1 TISNW

#2 RETISG

#3 AEBSRV

#4 REOISOL

#5 AMINSRL

#6 RREESWB

Arrange the circled letters to solve the mystery answer.

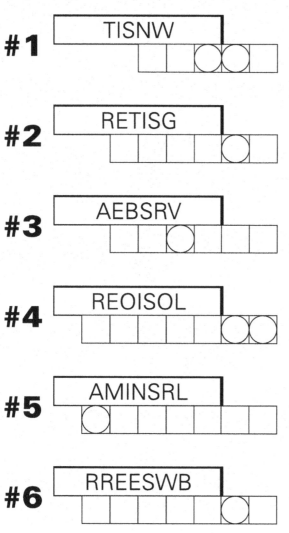

Interesting Baseball Facts

Joe Tinker of the Chicago Cubs was the first player to steal home twice in one game (1910).

Major league baseballs have a small cork core wound with more than 300 yards of wool yarn.

MYSTERY ANSWER

ALL ABOUT TREES

JUMBLE BrainBusters™

Unscramble the Jumbles, one letter to each square, to spell words related to trees.

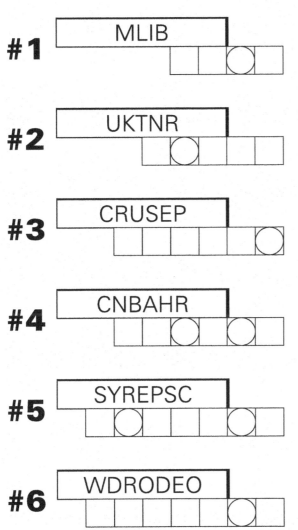

#1 MLIB

#2 UKTNR

#3 CRUSEP

#4 CNBAHR

#5 SYREPSC

#6 WDRODEO

Interesting Tree Facts

There are some palm tree seeds that can weigh up to 30 pounds.

During the typical growing season, a mature oak tree gives off thousands of gallons of moisture.

Arrange the circled letters to solve the mystery answer.

MYSTERY ANSWER

SUPER JUMBLE® CHALLENGE

JUMBLE BrainBusters™

#1 YDR

Unscramble the Jumbles, one letter to each square, to spell words.

#2 RBKA

#3 EMYRC

#4 RIOFLC

#5 SENCUER

#6 NIDILEGT

#7 VAEAILBAL

#8 APECEILYLS

#9 NPITDENENED

Box of Clues

Stumped? Maybe you can find a clue below.

-Part of a tree
  -Home to about 12 million
    -A condemning judgment
      -Steadily persevering
        -Compassion
          -Parched
            -Play
              -Particularly
                -Self-governing
                  -Obtainable

Arrange the circled letters to solve the mystery answer.

MYSTERY ANSWER

JUMBLE TRIVIA

Unscramble the Jumbles, one letter to each square, to spell words as suggested by the trivia clues.

#1 This word was added to dictionaries in the 1600s.

YCNAOR

#2 The ____ ____ lies at about 1,300 feet below sea level.

SEDEADA

#3 This man became U.S. president after the death of Warren G. Harding.

GLOCIODE

#4 There are more than 60 million _____ _____ books in print.

TESATRRK

#5 Logizomechanophobia is the fear of _____.

RTCOUPESM

Arrange the circled letters to solve the mystery answer.

The American _____ _____ was organized in 1881.

MYSTERY ANSWER

FIND THE JUMBLES®

Unscramble the Jumbles, one letter to each square, to spell words.

#1 ACCOH

#2 RITLEP

#3 TBATRE

#4 NSASEO

#5 ULBDOE

#6 NSICRGO

#7 UDSTMIA

#8 AGMNERA

Find and circle the answers (from above) in the grid of letters below.

```
T E G H R D S C O R I N G O I S
T H U I O P O R S T U O P R D T
Y R L U L F P U F E D C X N X A
H O I N M B I H B R E T O O P D
B U I P Y V C R B L N I O S B I
F O R N L A T I O R E W N A B U
T R T U O E O P I U P P L E H M
U G N C M A N A G E R N I S N O
H I H B A T T E R O P J K L O L
```

JUMBLE RIDDLES

JUMBLE BrainBusters™

Unscramble the mixed up letters to
reveal the punch lines to the riddles.

#1 What large instrument do
you carry in your ears?

SRUDM

#2 Who makes up jokes about
knitting?

IAITWTN

#3 What fish sings songs?

THUFAIANS

#4 What keeps out bugs and
shows movies?

RCESENS

#5 What is a musical pickle?

POCAIOLC

#6 What do you lose every
time you stand up?

AOURYLP

MATH

JUMBLE. BrainBusters™

Unscramble the Jumbles,
one letter to each square, so
that each equation is correct.

For example:

NONTEOEOW

ONE + ONE = TWO

#1

NNEOOEENO

☐☐◯ × ◯◯☐ = ☐◯☐

#2

VEFFNVEITIE

☐◯☐☐ + ☐☐◯☐ = ☐◯☐

#3

WSFIETOENVEV

☐☐☐◯ + ☐☐☐☐ = ◯☐☐☐☐☐

#4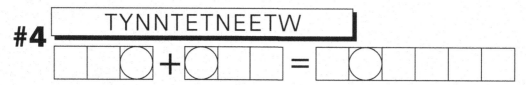

TYNNTETNEETW

☐☐◯☐ + ◯☐☐ = ☐◯☐☐☐

Then arrange the
circled letters to solve
the mystery equation.

MYSTERY EQUATION

◯◯◯◯◯ + ◯◯◯◯ = ◯◯◯◯

RHYMES WITH . . .

Unscramble the Jumbles, one letter to each square, to spell words that will each have a corresponding rhyming clue.

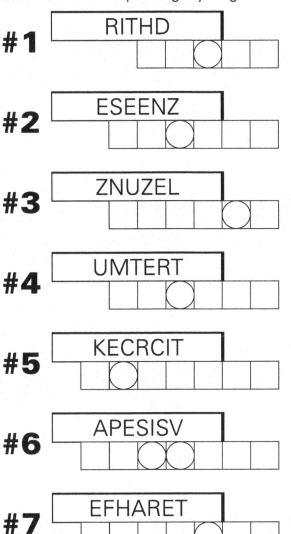

#1 RITHD

#2 ESEENZ

#3 ZNUZEL

#4 UMTERT

#5 KECRCIT

#6 APESISV

#7 EFHARET

GO - - - NO
TON - - - FUN
BACK - - - STACK
STUCK - - - TRUCK
MISTER - - - SISTER
SCANDAL - - - SANDAL

Box of Clues

Stumped? Maybe you can find a clue below.

-Rhymes with *ticket*
-Rhymes with *sputter*
-Rhymes with *muzzle*
-Rhymes with *leather*
-Rhymes with *heard*
-Rhymes with *breeze*
-Rhymes with *withers*
-Rhymes with *massive*

Arrange the circled letters to solve the mystery answer.

MYSTERY ANSWER

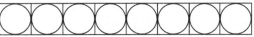

JUMBLE® CONNECTIONS

Unscramble the Jumbles, one letter to each square, to spell words that fit into the puzzle below.

ACROSS

- #1 EWINDLD
- #5 REGAGA
- #7 LIBAI
- #8 HLEBMIS
- #10 OEMV
- #12 UPEALGR
- #13 SNEITV

DOWN

- #1 AIDSMR
- #2 ENIBLM
- #3 PXELE
- #4 SROSG
- #5 AMGMA
- #6 HETINCG
- #8 BASPSY
- #9 OHOLWL
- #11 SIOSA

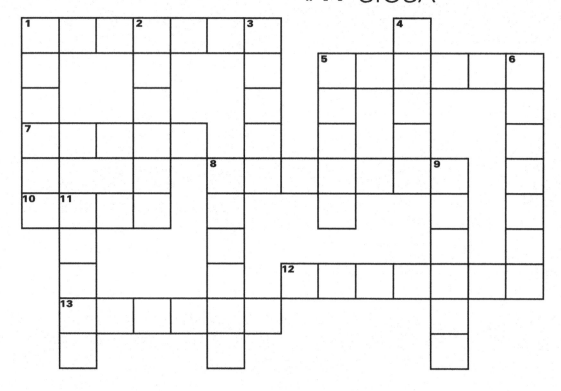

SUPER JUMBLE® CHALLENGE

#1 XTA

Unscramble the Jumbles, one letter to each square, to spell words.

#2 LHDO

#3 APOIN

#4 LJOTES

#5 UMFLFRE

#6 TATALFIY

#7 XOOIONBUS

#8 ONCFEENRCE

#9 FIGENTRPINR

Box of Clues

Stumped? Maybe you can find a clue below.

-Part of an exhaust system
-Make one's way by pushing
-Grasp
-Type of impression
-_____ call
-Businesslike
-Income _____
-Offensive
-Death
-Grand _____

Arrange the circled letters to solve the mystery answer.

MYSTERY ANSWER

FIND THE JUMBLES®

Unscramble the Jumbles, one letter
to each square, to spell words.

#1 TRKNU

#2 HWELE

#3 NENGIE

#4 ERNDEF

#5 BEUPRM

#6 AUBHCP

#7 RTBATEY

#8 TRDAOIRA

Find and circle the answers (from above) in the grid of letters below.

```
A V B C D T L F O I N M R E R O
W Y P N E E G X E Z B C R U T H
D H U R N A E F I N H J V E T U
Y R E I R P G J R E D T P K N B
P O G E U O N P O E F E N P M C
G N H O L T T P E R P U R G T A
E R A D I A T O R I R T R O P P
P B U M P E R F Y T N U P P O J
F U E N T E U B A T T E R Y G Y
```

SPORTS

Unscramble the Jumbles, one letter to each square, to spell words related to sports.

#1 YRBUG

#2 ROERR

#3 AHCCO

#4 SIKGIN

#5 EMLHET

#6 YARWFIA

Arrange the circled letters to solve the mystery answer.

Interesting Sports Facts

An official National Hockey League puck must measure 1 inch thick, be 3 inches in diameter, and weigh between 5½ and 6 ounces.

The first golf balls were made out of wood, as were the clubs.

MYSTERY ANSWER

MUSICAL INSTRUMENTS

Unscramble the Jumbles, one letter to each square, to spell names of musical instruments.

#1 OOEB

#2 RDSMU

#3 LIVION

#4 TUGIRA

#5 GBPISPAE

#6 MTOROEBN

Box of Clues

Stumped? Maybe you can find a clue below.

-Starts with *D*; ends with *S*

-Starts with *T*; ends with *E*

-Starts with *O*; ends with *E*

-Starts with *B*; ends with *S*

-Starts with *G*; ends with *R*

-Starts with *B*; ends with *N*

-Starts with *V*; ends with *N*

Arrange the circled letters to solve the mystery answer.

MYSTERY ANSWER

MEANS THE OPPOSITE

JUMBLE
BrainBusters™

Unscramble the Jumbles, one letter to each square, to spell pairs of words that have opposite or nearly opposite meanings.

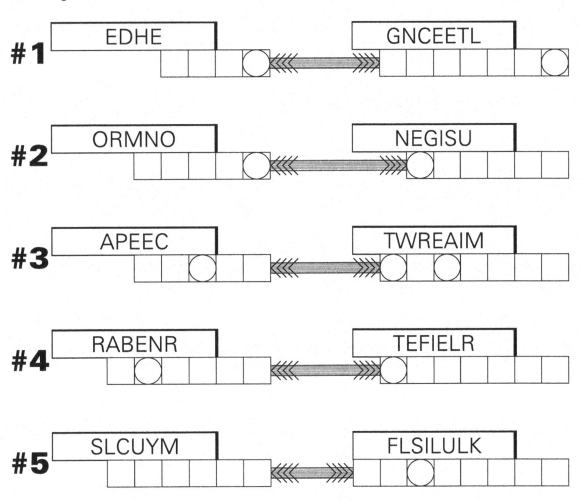

#1 EDHE — GNCEETL

#2 ORMNO — NEGISU

#3 APEEC — TWREAIM

#4 RABENR — TEFIELR

#5 SLCUYM — FLSILULK

Arrange the circled letters to solve the mystery answer.

MYSTERY
ANSWER

puzzle
47

FIND THE JUMBLES

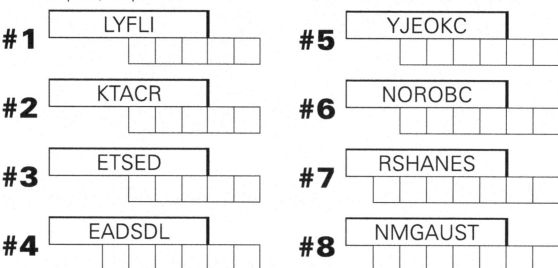

Unscramble the Jumbles, one letter
to each square, to spell words.

#1 LYFLI

#2 KTACR

#3 ETSED

#4 EADSDL

#5 YJEOKC

#6 NOROBC

#7 RSHANES

#8 NMGAUST

Find and circle the answers (from above) in the grid of letters below.

```
R X Z F O U M Z X H J P U I C L
S Y D F Y N H U P G U O P Z S P
S A P T H F L E S O N F C E T P
E T P O R U O Y O T U U I K E J
N T I U L A L P P S A D D L E K
R D P G E L C J O J O N I K D Y
A Y X R I L B K L B X T G L P O
H U K F U Z W I V H T S Y C L Z
L Z U R Y T U X B R O N C O H O
```

BASEBALL

Unscramble the Jumbles, one letter to each square, to spell words related to baseball.

#1 TICPH

#2 HCOCA

#3 GSIENL

#4 EGAELU

#5 BLOEDU

#6 LPFYOFA

Interesting Baseball Facts

A baseball hit by a metal bat can travel as fast as 120 miles per hour.

In 1934, Babe Ruth paid a fan $20 dollars for the return of the baseball he hit for his 700th career home run.

Arrange the circled letters to solve the mystery answer.

MYSTERY ANSWER

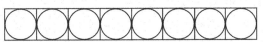

STARTS AND ENDS WITH THE SAME LETTER

Unscramble the Jumbles, one letter to each square, to spell words that start and end with the same letter.

#1 LTOITE

#2 RHUAHR

#3 LTEARIL

#4 ASCILSC

#5 TMRETON

#6 XAMIMMU

RADAR
ARENA POP GOING
RIVER HIGH
DICED CRYPTIC

Box of Clues

Stumped? Maybe you can find a clue below.

- Yippee
- Torture
- Verbatim
- Defense _____
- Vintage
- Greatest, largest
- _____ paper

Arrange the circled letters to solve the mystery answer.

MYSTERY ANSWER

PLANET EARTH

Unscramble the Jumbles, one letter to each square, to spell words related to planet Earth.

#1 EIRRV

#2 BHCAE

#3 WMSPA

#4 NTRCHE

#5 NURODG

Box of Clues

Stumped? Maybe you can find a clue below.

- Starts with *V*; ends with *O*
- Starts with *R*; ends with *R*
- Starts with *G*; ends with *D*
- Starts with *B*; ends with *H*
- Starts with *S*; ends with *P*
- Starts with *M*; ends with *N*
- Starts with *T*; ends with *H*

#6 NOLCAOV

Arrange the circled letters to solve the mystery answer.

MYSTERY ANSWER

SPORTS

Unscramble the Jumbles, one letter to each square, to spell words related to sports.

#1 GHFIT

#2 LTPRIE

#3 NINGIN

#4 NSNTIE

#5 YKCHOE

#6 EULFBM

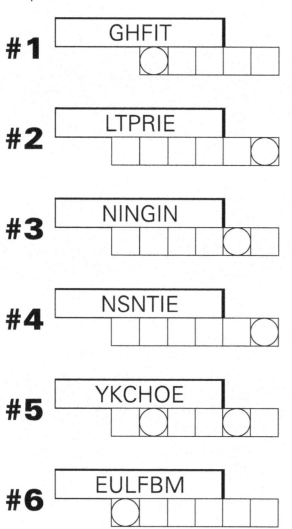

Box of Clues

Stumped? Maybe you can find a clue below.

-Baseball increment
-Table _____
-Bout
-Field _____
-At bat, in baseball
-Football mistake
-Baseball hit

Arrange the circled letters to solve the mystery answer.

MYSTERY ANSWER

WARS AND THE MILITARY

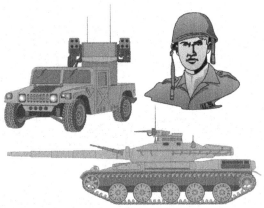

Unscramble the Jumbles, one letter to each square, to spell words related to wars and the military.

#1 GTERTA

#2 NCONNA

#3 THEELM

#4 UASARIM

#5 TICAPNA

#6 ARWEARF

Box of Clues

Stumped? Maybe you can find a clue below.

-Type of warrior
-_____ practice
-Military operations between enemies
-Large, heavy gun
-Means of concealment
-Military rank
-Protective covering

Arrange the circled letters to solve the mystery answer.

MYSTERY ANSWER

MEANS THE SAME

JUMBLE BrainBusters™

Unscramble the Jumbles, one letter
to each square, to spell pairs of words
that have the same or similar meanings.

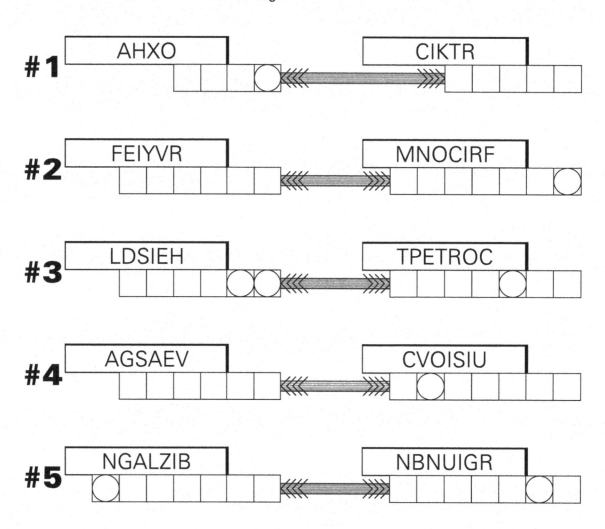

#1 AHXO — CIKTR

#2 FEIYVR — MNOCIRF

#3 LDSIEH — TPETROC

#4 AGSAEV — CVOISIU

#5 NGALZIB — NBNUIGR

Arrange the circled letters to solve the mystery answer.

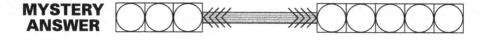

MYSTERY ANSWER

JUMBLE® CONNECTIONS

Unscramble the Jumbles, one letter to each square, to spell words that fit into the puzzle below.

ACROSS

- #1 BSVIOUO
- #5 VGLARU
- #7 TIORB
- #8 ESLTEPE
- #10 AGGN
- #12 RFGOEIN
- #13 SPIONO

DOWN

- #1 OGLBNO
- #2 NGININ
- #3 HTGIS
- #4 ALIFL
- #5 TAVLE
- #6 ENUNRIO
- #8 UOMSMN
- #9 SEMKIO
- #11 DTOAP

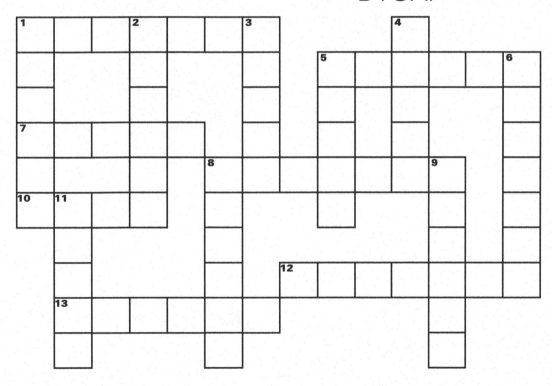

ABBREVIATIONS

Unscramble the Jumbles, one letter to each square, to spell words that are often abbreviated.

#1 EAUVEN

#2 UATGSU

#3 DSYNAU

#4 RUMNBE

#5 GIVEENN

#6 BRUERAYF

Arrange the circled letters to solve the mystery answer.

Sec.
Frwy. Dup.
Ave. Feb.
Ref.
Diam. Dist.
Dec.
Aug.
Bldg.
No.
Oct. Sept.
Lbs.
Blvd.
Tkt. Eve.
Sun.
Capt.
Oz.

MYSTERY ANSWER

STARTS WITH AND ENDS WITH A VOWEL

Unscramble the Jumbles, one letter to each square, to spell words that start with and end with a vowel.

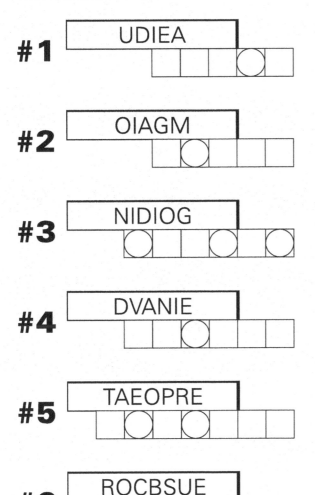

#1 UDIEA

#2 OIAGM

#3 NIDIOG

#4 DVANIE

#5 TAEOPRE

#6 ROCBSUE

Arrange the circled letters to solve the mystery answer.

Box of Clues

Stumped? Maybe you can find a clue below.

-Spread over or into
-Friend
-Deep reddish blue
-Arrange offhand
-Run
-Remote, secluded
-Farewell

MYSTERY ANSWER

BIRDS

JUMBLE BrainBusters™

Unscramble the Jumbles, one letter to each square, to spell varieties of birds.

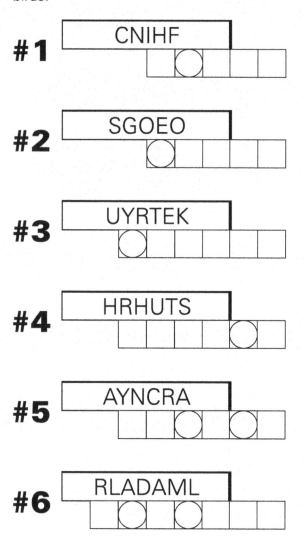

#1 CNIHF

#2 SGOEO

#3 UYRTEK

#4 HRHUTS

#5 AYNCRA

#6 RLADAML

Interesting Bird Facts

The smallest bird is the hummingbird. Some are so small that one of their enemies is the praying mantis.

Albatrosses lay the heaviest eggs of any seabird

Macaws are the largest and most colorful species of parrot.

Arrange the circled letters to solve the mystery answer.

MYSTERY ANSWER

RHYMES WITH . . .

JUMBLE BrainBusters™

Unscramble the Jumbles, one letter to each square, to spell words that will each have a corresponding rhyming clue.

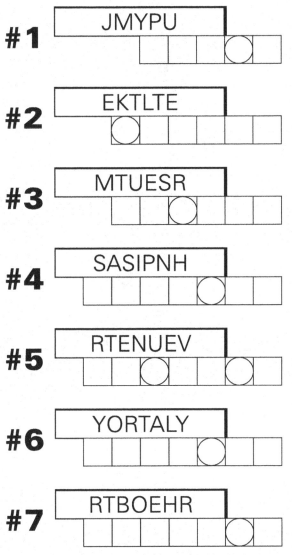

#1 JMYPU

#2 EKTLTE

#3 MTUESR

#4 SASIPNH

#5 RTENUEV

#6 YORTALY

#7 RTBOEHR

GO · · · NO
TON · · · FUN
BACK · · · STACK
STUCK · · · TRUCK
MISTER · · · SISTER
SCANDAL · · · SANDAL

Box of Clues

Stumped? Maybe you can find a clue below.

-Rhymes with *smother*
-Rhymes with *banish*
-Rhymes with *lumpy*
-Rhymes with *denture*
-Rhymes with *twinkle*
-Rhymes with *mettle*
-Rhymes with *luster*
-Rhymes with *loyalty*

Arrange the circled letters to solve the mystery answer.

MYSTERY ANSWER

JUMBLE RIDDLES

Unscramble the mixed up letters to
reveal the punch lines to the riddles.

#1 What has a neck but no
head?

LTABTEO

#2 What goes further the
slower it goes?

EYOMN

#3 What can have a hundred
limbs but can't walk?

ETARE

#4 What "bus" crossed the
ocean?

MUSOLCBU

#5 The alphabet goes from
A to Z. What goes from
Z to A?

AEBZR

#6 What fish do knights eat?

WIOSRHSDF

JUMBLE®

BrainBusters™

Intermediate Puzzles

puzzle 60

ANIMALS

Unscramble the Jumbles, one letter to each square, to spell names of animals.

#1 HIORN

#2 HCPIM

#3 ELMRU

#4 YKTUER

#5 POGRHE

#6 ETHCAEH

Box of Clues

Stumped? Maybe you can find a clue below.

- Starts with *L*; ends with *R*
- Starts with *R*; ends with *O*
- Starts with *T*; ends with *Y*
- Starts with *P*; ends with *E*
- Starts with *C*; ends with *H*
- Starts with *C*; ends with *P*
- Starts with *G*; ends with *R*

Arrange the circled letters to solve the mystery answer.

MYSTERY ANSWER

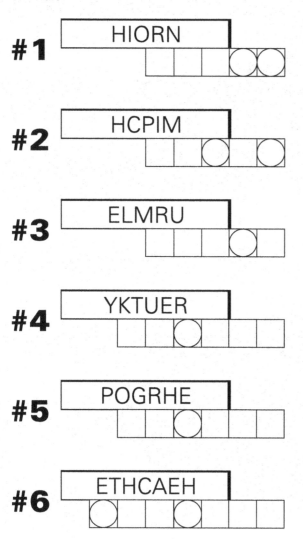

THE NAME GAME

Unscramble the Jumbles, one letter
to each square, to spell last names,
as suggested by the first name clues.

Lee _____, born in 1924
#1 CICOAAC

William _____, born in 1931
#2 NASTRHE

Andy _____, born in 1919
#3 NEROYO

Peggy _____, born in 1948
#4 EFIMGNL

Michael _____, born in 1963
#5 DJRNAO

Bill _____, born in 1937
#6 BCSYO

Dick _____, born in 1941
#7 NEECYH

Jack _____, born in 1940
#8 UANKLSIC

Diane _____, born in 1945
#9 ESYRAW

Andy _____, born in 1927
#10 LILWISMA

ALL ABOUT FOOD

Unscramble the Jumbles, one letter to each square, to spell words related to food.

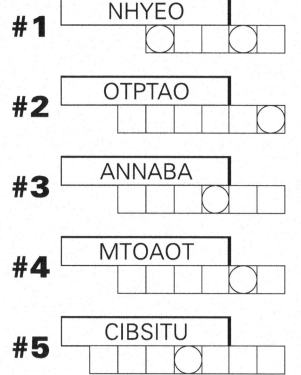

#1 NHYEO

#2 OTPTAO

#3 ANNABA

#4 MTOAOT

#5 CIBSITU

#6 KECARRC

#7 TOPLYUR

Interesting Food Facts

There are thousands of varieties of apples.

Goats' milk is used more widely throughout the world than cows' milk.

Olive oil is made from green olives.

Arrange the circled letters to solve the mystery answer.

MYSTERY ANSWER

FIND THE JUMBLES

Unscramble the Jumbles, one letter to each square, to spell words.

#1 ENCIE

#2 CENUL

#3 BHUYB

#4 RATFEH

#5 ONUSIC

#6 NUHSBAD

#7 HAUDGETR

#8 DRAGNOSN

Find and circle the answers (from above) in the grid of letters below.

```
P F U I O H R D A U G H T E R U
U R E T Y U U R F V H N K O L P
T F E T C D I B N G O P T U P N
H U N J K E U P B S P O R I O N
K G P E L T R U D Y I E P O M I
N U T C O J H N T U H P J L P S
G R N E R E A Y U T U P U L P U
R U L I F R R K A L Y L J B O O
F Y T N G C T F H U S B A N D C
```

ADJECTIVES

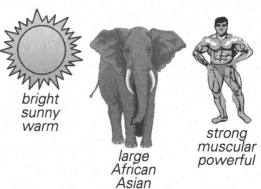

JUMBLE BrainBusters™

Unscramble the Jumbles, one letter
to each square, to spell adjectives.

#1 TRUYS

#2 NWNOK

#3 RHRIDO

#4 OYNRER

#5 XTEITNC

#6 ALBLVOE

#7 YNOBATU

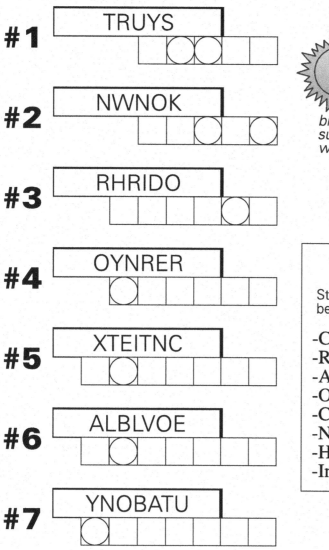

bright
sunny
warm

large
African
Asian

strong
muscular
powerful

Box of Clues

Stumped? Maybe you can find a clue
below.

-Cranky
-Recognized
-Attracting affection
-Out of practice
-Capable of floating
-No longer existing
-Highly offensive
-Inspiring disgust

Arrange the circled letters
to solve the mystery answer.

MYSTERY ANSWER

SUPER JUMBLE® CHALLENGE

JUMBLE® BrainBusters™

#1 EBE

Unscramble the Jumbles, one letter to each square, to spell words.

#2 USRL

#3 FNILA

#4 SFIHIN

#5 OIUTRNE

#6 NKNDILIG

#7 ESSNEEMGR

#8 HNOENMPEON

#9 ABERMARSEDS

Box of Clues

Stumped? Maybe you can find a clue below.

-Regular course of procedure
-Last
-Combustible material
-Significant fact or event
-Irritable
-_____ line
-Spelling _____
-Ashamed, rattled
-Make indistinct
-Dispatch bearer

Arrange the circled letters to solve the mystery answer.

MYSTERY ANSWER

U.S. STATE CAPITALS

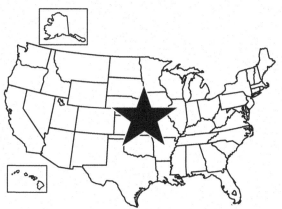

Unscramble the Jumbles, one letter to each square, to spell names of U.S. state capitals.

#1 ENHLAE

#2 NUJAUE

#3 IGARHLE

#4 SAOJNKC

#5 KASRBCIM

#6 BUSOUMCL

Box of Clues

Stumped? Maybe you can find a clue below. (No clue for the mystery answer.)

-Starts with *J*; ends with *U*

-Starts with *C*; ends with *S*

-Starts with *H*; ends with *A*

-Starts with *R*; ends with *H*

-Starts with *B*; ends with *K*

-Starts with *J*; ends with *N*

Arrange the circled letters to solve the mystery answer.

MYSTERY ANSWER

ALL ABOUT MUSIC

JUMBLE BrainBusters™

Unscramble the Jumbles, one letter to each square, to spell words related to music.

#1 PRAH

#2 RHON

#3 ODRCH

#4 MDOEYL

#5 MPTRTEU

#6 ORNAHYM

Box of Clues

Stumped? Maybe you can find a clue below.

-Instrument with a flared end
-Musical agreement of sounds
-Song
-Group of notes played together
-Stringed instrument
-_____ section
-French _____

Arrange the circled letters to solve the mystery answer.

MYSTERY ANSWER

BASKETBALL

Unscramble the Jumbles, one letter
to each square, to spell words related
to basketball.

#1 UOLF

#2 RDAUG

#3 TSBEKA

#4 LEBDIRB

#5 FENEFSO

#6 MRFUION

Interesting Basketball Fact

According to basketball
manufacturer Spalding, the
average life span of an NBA
basketball is about forty
thousand to fifty thousand
bounces.

The first basketball rules book
was published in 1892.

Arrange the circled letters
to solve the mystery answer.

MYSTERY ANSWER

JUMBLE RIDDLES

Unscramble the mixed up letters to reveal the punch lines to the riddles.

#1 Dogs have fleas. What do sheep have?

LEFECE

#2 What kind of tables do people eat?

EBEETALVSG

#3 What flower is happiest?

LAGDIOAAL

#4 What kind of pine has the sharpest needles?

PORACUINEP

#5 Who settled in the West before anyone else?

UHETSN

#6 What insect curses in a low voice?

SLOCATU

JUMBLE® CONNECTIONS

Unscramble the Jumbles, one letter to each square, to spell words that fit into the puzzle below.

JUMBLE BrainBusters™

ACROSS

#1 UNSORIH
#5 WRFURO
#7 URRMO
#8 KORFSAE
#10 VOEW
#12 LESPICA
#13 ESODXU

DOWN

#1 ORNARW
#2 PEORSE
#3 LHLOE
#4 KCWER
#5 SFUHL
#6 USHWIFL
#8 UFSNGU
#9 QEYTIU
#11 ROERD

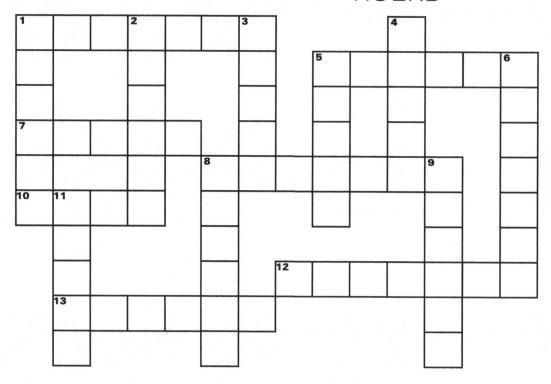

SUPER JUMBLE® CHALLENGE

JUMBLE® BrainBusters™

#1 NCA

Unscramble the Jumbles, one letter to each square, to spell words.

#2 MIFL

#3 BLOBY

#4 SPLIHO

#5 HASAEMD

#6 PLDOMITA

#7 SDSPLEIEA

#8 MRAICLUSUO

#9 SPIESIMISTC

Box of Clues
Stumped? Maybe you can find a clue below.

-Part of a theater
-Make smooth and glossy
-Tactful negotiator
-Fire
-Bring to completion
-Negative
-To fail to satisfy
-Marvelous
-Feeling guilt
-Motion picture

Arrange the circled letters to solve the mystery answer.

MYSTERY ANSWER

JUMBLE RIDDLES

Unscramble the mixed up letters to
reveal the punch lines to the riddles.

#1 What is the brightest fish?

UHASINFS

#2 What do you call cattle
that sit on the grass?

ROEUGNBEDF

#3 What did the tired shrub
say to the other shrub?

MABUISEDH

#4 What kind of person is
fed up with people?

NACNAIBLA

#5 What has a head, can't
think, but drives?

MHMEARA

#6 What lands as often on its
tail as it does on its head?

YENANP

ADVERBS

Unscramble the Jumbles, one letter
to each square, to spell adverbs.

#1  LEIAYS

#2  REYELF

#3  HOWLYL

#4 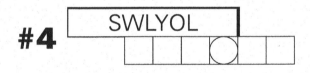 SWLYOL

#5 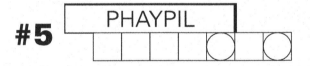 PHAYPIL

#6  GIGYERLN

The runner ran <u>quickly</u>.
The runner ran <u>slowly</u>.

Box of Clues

Stumped? Maybe you can find a clue
below. (No clue for the mystery answer.)

-Without speed
-Entirely
-With pleasure
-Without difficulty
-Without restrictions
-Carefully

Arrange the circled letters
to solve the mystery answer.

MYSTERY ANSWER

ADJECTIVES

Unscramble the Jumbles, one letter to each square, to spell adjectives.

#1 NFYUN

#2 ARWEY

#3 YLEIVL

#4 RBGOIN

#5 EADODR

#6 VDEUTO

#7 OYOSUJ

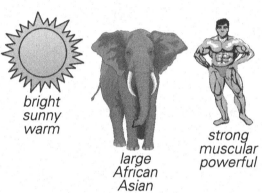

bright
sunny
warm

large
African
Asian

strong
muscular
powerful

Box of Clues

Stumped? Maybe you can find a clue below.

- Energetic
- Happy
- Fantastic
- Serious, earnest
- Dull
- Loved
- Humorous
- Exhausted

Arrange the circled letters to solve the mystery answer.

MYSTERY ANSWER

SPORTS

Unscramble the Jumbles, one letter
to each square, to spell words related
to sports.

#1 TMTI

#2 HCTAC

#3 EKRTIS

#4 EYESJR

#5 DULDHE

#6 RPECHIT

JUMBLE® Trivia Quick Quiz

In what U.S. city do all
the major sports teams
wear the same colors?

HISTUBRPGT

ANSWER:

Arrange the circled letters
to solve the mystery answer.

MYSTERY ANSWER

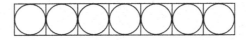

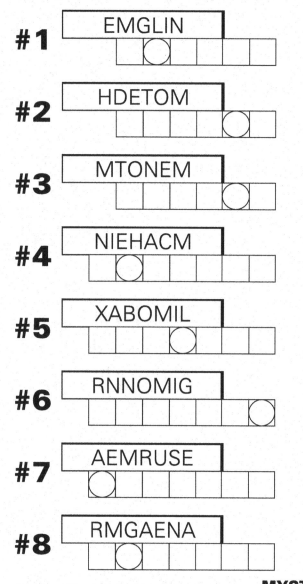

STARTS WITH M

Unscramble the Jumbles, one letter to each square, to spell words that start with *M*.

#1 EMGLIN

#2 HDETOM

#3 MTONEM

#4 NIEHACM

#5 XABOMIL

#6 RNNOMIG

#7 AEMRUSE

#8 RMGAENA

Arrange the circled letters to solve the mystery answer.

JUMBLE BrainBusters™

MMMMMM
MMMMMM
MMMMMM
MMMMMM

Box of Clues

Stumped? Maybe you can find a clue below.

-Part of the day
-Ascertain the extent of
-Mix
-Head coach in baseball
-Letter container
-Type of tree
-Instant
-Washing _____
-Systematic procedure

MYSTERY ANSWER

MAMMALS

Unscramble the Jumbles, one letter to each square, to spell names of mammals.

#1 NPAAD

#2 LHSOT

#3 REEFTR

#4 AGARJU

#5 YCOOET

#6 ESAWLE

#7 GLMINEM

Arrange the circled letters to solve the mystery answer.

Interesting Mammal Facts

A baby giraffe is approximately 6 feet tall at birth.

Hippos are born underwater.

A baby blue whale is approximately 25 feet long at birth.

MYSTERY ANSWER

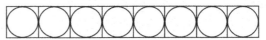

MATH

JUMBLE BrainBusters™

Unscramble the Jumbles,
one letter to each square, so
that each equation is correct.

For example:

NONTEOEOW
ONE + ONE = TWO

#1 OWFTVETEIN

☐☐◯☐ × ◯☐☐ = ☐☐☐

#2 TESVNENNOEIW

☐◯☐◯☐ + ☐◯☐☐ = ☐◯☐☐

#3 RFOZUOFURORE

◯☐☐☐☐ − ◯☐☐☐ = ☐☐☐☐

#4 TXSFIYTNEIYTF

☐◯◯☐☐ + ☐☐◯☐ = ☐☐☐☐◯

Then arrange the
circled letters to solve
the mystery equation.

MYSTERY EQUATION

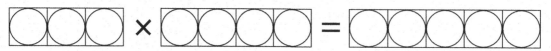

◯◯◯ × ◯◯◯◯◯ = ◯◯◯◯◯◯

THE NAME GAME

JUMBLE
BrainBusters™

Unscramble the Jumbles, one letter to each square, to spell last names, as suggested by the first name clues.

Pat _____, born in 1934

#1 ONBEO

John _____, born in 1953

#2 RDEDASW

Hillary _____, born in 1947

#3 COTINNL

Susan _____, born in 1946

#4 DRAOSNNA

Roger _____, born in 1962

#5 MCEELSN

Kate _____, born in 1975

#6 LINEWTS

Harry _____, born in 1923

#7 NEESORAR

Wayne _____, born in 1961

#8 TZGKYRE

Paul _____, born in 1918

#9 RVAEYH

Tom _____, born in 1945

#10 LCSEKLE

RHYMES WITH . . .

Unscramble the Jumbles, one letter to each square, to spell words that will each have a corresponding rhyming clue.

#1 TBTREU

#2 HNTERC

#3 FATERUE

#4 CTLARTE

#5 EWALHTY

#6 LGOMRAU

#7 EWDLESES

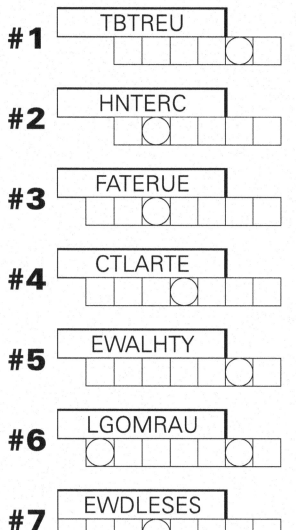

JUMBLE BrainBusters™

GO - - - NO
TON - - - FUN
BACK - - - STACK
STUCK - - - TRUCK
MISTER - - - SISTER
SCANDAL - - - SANDAL

Box of Clues

Stumped? Maybe you can find a clue below.

-Rhymes with *wrench*
-Rhymes with *clamor*
-Rhymes with *needless*
-Rhymes with *cutter*
-Rhymes with *healthy*
-Rhymes with *splatter*
-Rhymes with *slaughter*
-Rhymes with *creature*

Arrange the circled letters to solve the mystery answer.

MYSTERY ANSWER

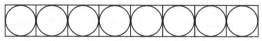

SUPER JUMBLE® CHALLENGE

#1 PNU

Unscramble the Jumbles, one letter to each square, to spell words.

#2 RPUR

#3 NBLDO

#4 LBALTO

#5 XTETREU

#6 EKEPSKEA

#7 PEBSERADD

#8 ETIMCULUSO

#9 HRSHOTNAEDD

Box of Clues
Stumped? Maybe you can find a clue below.

-Of a pale, yellowish brown color
-The feel of a surface
-In need of more people
-Ornamental cloth cover
-Humorous use of a word
-Careful
-A reason to take cover
-Memento
-_____ box
-Cat sound

Arrange the circled letters to solve the mystery answer.

MYSTERY ANSWER

JUMBLE® CONNECTIONS

Unscramble the Jumbles, one letter to each
square, to spell words that fit into the puzzle
below.

JUMBLE BrainBusters™

ACROSS

#1 PDOUNIM
#5 HWMART
#7 XFFIA
#8 NAFOTRF
#10 YUTD
#12 UCONCTO
#13 MLGOAJ

DOWN

#1 AIDNLN
#2 TODIYD
#3 RDWFA
#4 NOFWR
#5 LWRHI
#6 HOAFYLT
#8 CAULTA
#9 NTGEIW
#11 UECLN

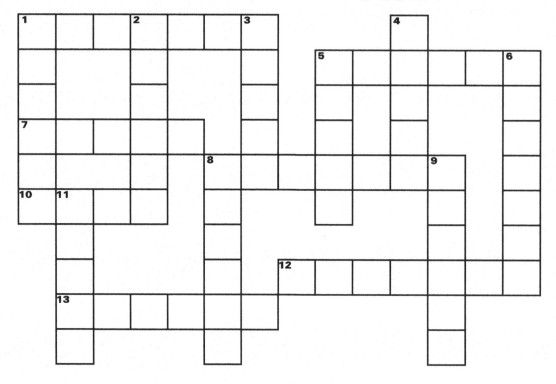

84

ABBREVIATIONS

JUMBLE
BrainBusters™

Unscramble the Jumbles, one letter to each square, to spell words that are often abbreviated.

#1 TCTKIE

#2 ACPITNA

#3 ROTCBEO

#4 EFREYAW

#5 CITRDSIT

#6 ULBINDIG

Sec.
Frwy.
Dup.
Ave.
Feb.
Ref.
Diam.
Dist.
Dec.
Aug.
Bldg.
No.
Oct.
Sept.
Lbs.
Blvd.
Sun.
Tkt.
Eve.
Oz.
Capt.

Arrange the circled letters to solve the mystery answer.

MYSTERY ANSWER

FIND THE JUMBLES

Unscramble the Jumbles, one letter
to each square, to spell words.

#1 ASLAS

#2 PALKO

#3 TALZW

#4 ASBMA

#5 MBMAO

#6 FOTORXT

#7 GNOAFDNA

#8 RBAOLOLM

Find and circle the answers (from above) in the grid of letters below.

```
A Z C Y G I X P R Y H L Z D D A
B S B A L L R O O M A V X H F N
N L A L O P U R Z U T O E J O H
O M K L K G L T S C B T L F X K
Z E L O S U L L U M P I G N T L
D C O F S A M B A J L Z S N R O
J B P B W H G M H T B D R O O Z
C G Z N C U N H K X V K G P T F
X C I C F A N D A N G O H P G Z
```

ALL ABOUT CHESS

Unscramble the Jumbles, one letter to each square, to spell words related to chess.

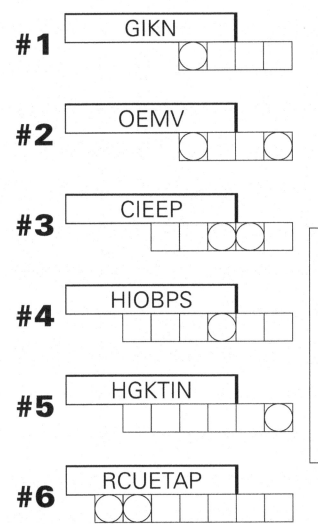

#1 GIKN

#2 OEMV

#3 CIEEP

#4 HIOBPS

#5 HGKTIN

#6 RCUETAP

Chess Q & A

QUESTION:
How many ways are there to play the first 10 moves in a game of chess?

ANSWER:
169,518,829,100,544,000

Arrange the circled letters to solve the mystery answer.

MYSTERY ANSWER

JUMBLE TRIVIA

Unscramble the Jumbles, one letter to each square, to spell words as suggested by the trivia clues.

#1 This manual computing device has been used in China since ancient times.

BAASCU

#2 The human body has approximately 45 miles of these.

SEVERN

#3 The country of Tonga once issued a stamp in the shape of a _____.

ANAABN

#4 This animal can weigh as much as 400 pounds.

THOCIRS

#5 It takes 120 drops of water to equal one _____.

APOTSONE

Arrange the circled letters to solve the mystery answer.

Dry ice does not melt; it does this.

MYSTERY ANSWER

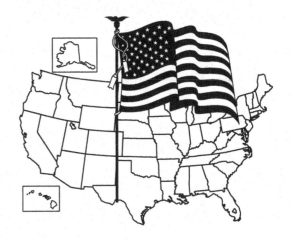

U.S. STATES

JUMBLE BrainBusters™

Unscramble the Jumbles, one letter to each square, to spell names of U.S. states.

#1 ADFOIRL

#2 ROVETMN

#3 HAIGMINC

#4 KTECYUNK

#5 OLCRADOO

#6 AHOLOAKM

#7 NICIOSNSW

Arrange the circled letters to solve the mystery answer.

Interesting U.S. State Facts

South Dakota's official state musical instrument is the fiddle.

In 1919, the pecan tree became the official state tree of Texas.

MYSTERY ANSWER

WEATHER

Unscramble the Jumbles, one letter to each square, to spell words related to weather.

#1 NUSYN

#2 LFODO

#3 YSTESM

#4 TDHUERN

#5 ANRWIGN

#6 NOSOMNO

Box of Clues

Stumped? Maybe you can find a clue below.

-Starts with *T*; ends with *R*

-Starts with *S*; ends with *Y*

-Starts with *M*; ends with *N*

-Starts with *S*; ends with *M*

-Starts with *W*; ends with *G*

-Starts with *S*; ends with *M*

-Starts with *F*; ends with *D*

Arrange the circled letters to solve the mystery answer.

MYSTERY ANSWER

90

SPORTS

Unscramble the Jumbles, one letter to each square, to spell words related to sports.

#1 OEVLG

#2 TSIENN

#3 ROKOIE

#4 LUBDEO

#5 FAYRWIA

#6 DADNMIO

Box of Clues

Stumped? Maybe you can find a clue below. (No clue for the mystery answer.)

-Mitt
-First-year player
-Golf-ball landing area
-Sport played on a court
-Bases' shape
-Baseball hit

Arrange the circled letters to solve the mystery answer.

MYSTERY ANSWER

JUMBLE RIDDLES

Unscramble the mixed up letters to reveal the punch lines to the riddles.

#1 What do you call a sunburn on your stomach?

OPTOARST

#2 What do liars do after they die?

LEISLTIL

#3 Who can marry a lot of wives and still be single?

NAISMRITE

#4 What do you call it when pigs do their laundry?

HAOHWSG

#5 What does Brazil produce that no other country produces?

ZRAILABNIS

#6 What goes up and never comes down?

UORAYGE

JUMBLE® TRIVIA

Unscramble the Jumbles, one letter to each square, to spell words as suggested by the trivia clues.

#1 This feline is a good swimmer and will sometimes catch fish for food.

UARJGA

#2 This animal eats crabs, lobsters, and other shellfish.

UPOTOSC

#3 This city, which is home to more than 400,000 people, is one of Japan's leading ports.

KNAAISAG

#4 Alexander _____ was born on the island of Nevis, in the West Indies, in 1755.

NOMHITLA

#5 _____ is the second-largest Central American country.

RDHOUASN

Arrange the circled letters to solve the mystery answer.

This political leader died on July 4, 1826.

MYSTERY ANSWER

93

SUPER JUMBLE® CHALLENGE

JUMBLE BrainBusters™

#1 CIY

Unscramble the Jumbles, one letter to each square, to spell words.

#2 YFIF

#3 AOMWN

#4 GDEITS

#5 CIAEEVH

#6 RCTOBSUT

#7 NCOWNUTDO

#8 CMSCOAPIHL

#9 EUOMTRIORIS

Box of Clues

Stumped? Maybe you can find a clue below.

- Condensation of information
- Time remaining
- Frozen and slick
- Complete
- Lady
- Reach
- Situation, condition
- Block
- Deserving of honor
- Uncertain

Arrange the circled letters to solve the mystery answer.

MYSTERY ANSWER ◯◯◯◯◯◯◯◯◯◯◯◯◯◯◯

JUMBLE CONNECTIONS

Unscramble the Jumbles, one letter to each square, to spell words that fit into the puzzle below.

ACROSS
- #1 TOPNPIG
- #5 RJUITS
- #7 YKAKA
- #8 NEMETMO
- #10 EULY
- #12 PIONINO
- #13 NGSEIU

DOWN
- #1 ETRKUY
- #2 PAEACL
- #3 LIGUE
- #4 RTUEP
- #5 JKEOR
- #6 HTOYPON
- #8 EGMORU
- #9 FCOFIE
- #11 AEGSU

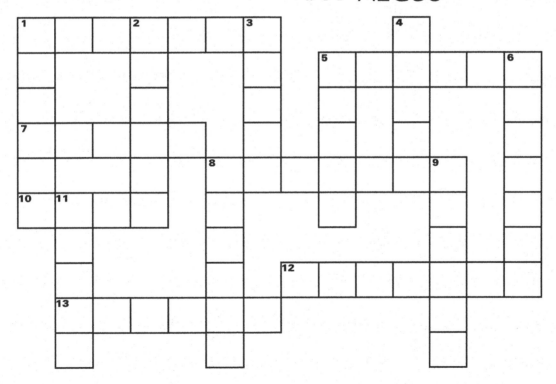

ALL ABOUT MONEY

Unscramble the Jumbles, one letter to each square, to spell words related to money.

#1 UVLAT

#2 NYEPN

#3 BRKENA

#4 AECRGH

#5 RLAODL

#6 ENMICO

Interesting Money Fact

The smallest monetary unit ever issued in the U.S. was the half cent. It was minted from 1793 through 1857.

Arrange the circled letters to solve the mystery answer.

MYSTERY ANSWER

RHYMES WITH . . .

Unscramble the Jumbles, one letter
to each square, to spell words that will
each have a corresponding rhyming clue.

JUMBLE BrainBusters™

#1 AIBRBT

#2 NJALGE

#3 TGLHILY

#4 PAPONIT

#5 OBTESMR

#6 NICFUTON

#7 TEHSANAP

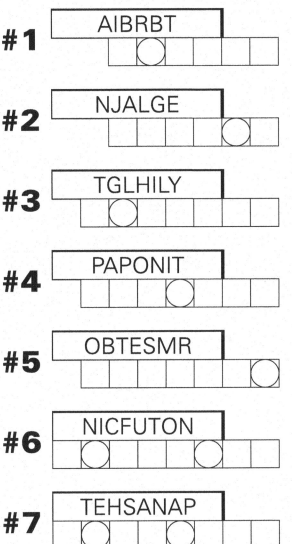

GO - - - NO
TON - - - FUN
BACK - - - STACK
STUCK - - - TRUCK
MISTER - - - SISTER
SCANDAL - - - SANDAL

Box of Clues

Stumped? Maybe you can find a clue
below.

-Rhymes with *mangle*
-Rhymes with *pleasant*
-Rhymes with *habit*
-Rhymes with *junction*
-Rhymes with *lobster*
-Rhymes with *anoint*
-Rhymes with *gregarious*
-Rhymes with *nightly*

Arrange the circled letters
to solve the mystery answer.

MYSTERY ANSWER

JUMBLE® TRIVIA

Unscramble the Jumbles, one letter to each square, to spell words as suggested by the trivia clues.

#1 Diane _____ is a member of the Television Academy of Fame.

WSAERY

#2 There are 900,000 known species of these.

CITSESN

#3 Five hundred young men auditioned for the lead roles on *The _____*.

KEMNESO

#4 John _____ was born on February 18, 1954, in Englewood, New Jersey.

LTOTARAV

#5 It is believed that this sport originated in India.

ODNABTNIM

Arrange the circled letters to solve the mystery answer.

This geographic region's name means "New Scotland."

MYSTERY ANSWER

ALL ABOUT TREES

JUMBLE BrainBusters™

Unscramble the Jumbles, one letter to each square, to spell words related to trees.

#1 EDLENE

#2 LIWLWO

#3 OBMOBA

#4 AGFIEOL

#5 OTCUONC

#6 WOGDODO

Box of Clues

Stumped? Maybe you can find a clue below.

-Weeping _____
-Pine _____
-Tree with white, yellow, rose, or purple flowers
-Hollow-stemmed wood
-Flowering tree that comes in pink and white varieties
-Leaves, flowers, and branches
-_____ palm

Arrange the circled letters to solve the mystery answer.

MYSTERY ANSWER

STARTS WITH R

JUMBLE
BrainBusters™

Unscramble the Jumbles, one letter to each square, to spell words that start with R.

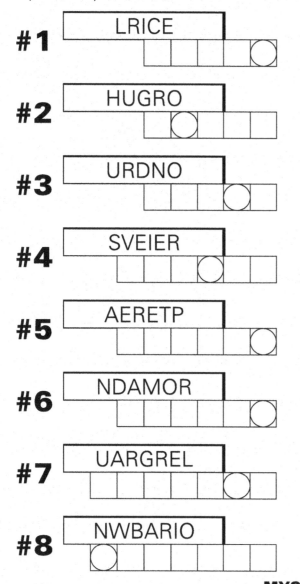

#1 LRICE

#2 HUGRO

#3 URDNO

#4 SVEIER

#5 AERETP

#6 NDAMOR

#7 UARGREL

#8 NWBARIO

R R R R R R
R R R R R R
R R R R R R
R R R R R R

Box of Clues

Stumped? Maybe you can find a clue below.

-Routine, normal
-Change
-Harsh
-Haphazard
-Circle's adjective
-Lovey-dovey
-Memento
-Colorful phenomenon
-Rerun

Arrange the circled letters to solve the mystery answer.

MYSTERY ANSWER

FIND THE JUMBLES

JUMBLE BrainBusters™

Unscramble the Jumbles, one letter to each square, to spell words.

#1 PCEHR

#2 UGPYP

#3 SNOLMA

#4 UBHAITL

#5 HCIODFS

#6 AIRNAHP

#7 OIGSLFDH

#8 RMLCEKEA

Find and circle the answers (from above) in the grid of letters below.

```
D C F E G H C O J U Z P K A L Y
H F A X D A U O F X P S H X P L
S Y Z H F L X J D H D N P Z E E
I N P I D I P Z D F A C Y H R R
F C Y F Y B O L T R I N V N C E
D C V P T U Y T I G N S P O H K
L B P P U T O P H L Z L H K U C
O U B S A L M O N L K N P B G A
G Y Z F E A C A N B X J N Z H M
```

STARTS AND ENDS WITH THE SAME LETTER

Unscramble the Jumbles, one letter to each square, to spell words that start and end with the same letter.

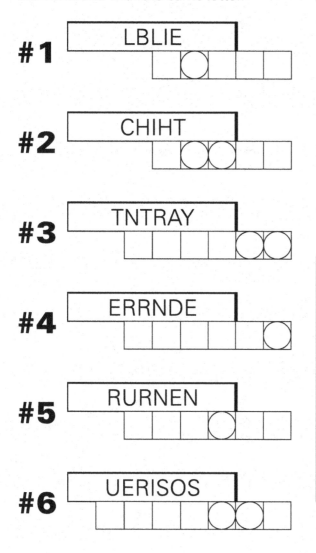

#1 LBLIE

#2 CHIHT

#3 TNTRAY

#4 ERRNDE

#5 RURNEN

#6 UERISOS

Box of Clues

Stumped? Maybe you can find a clue below.

-Trailer _____
-Slanderous statement
-Evil leader
-Solemn
-Maintaining process related to food
-Type of rug
-Transmit to another

Arrange the circled letters to solve the mystery answer.

MYSTERY ANSWER

THE NAME GAME

Unscramble the Jumbles, one letter to each square, to spell last names, as suggested by the first name clues.

Heather _____, born in 1961

#1 KLCEROLA

Michael _____, born in 1933

#2 AKDKISU

Ron _____, born in 1954

#3 RHAODW

Walter _____, born in 1916

#4 NCOITEKR

Jessica _____, born in 1909

#5 DTNYA

Linda _____, born in 1956

#6 MHILNAOT

Al _____, born in 1940

#7 NPIOCA

Billy _____, born in 1918

#8 HRAMAG

Paul _____, born in 1925

#9 WNANEM

Ed _____, born in 1941

#10 DBALYRE

SUPER JUMBLE® CHALLENGE

JUMBLE BrainBusters™

#1 MHU

Unscramble the Jumbles, one letter to each square, to spell words.

#2 RGWO

#3 OYHNE

#4 HTIERV

#5 TATEPTM

#6 GIMFUTEA

#7 NIVRETONY

#8 GHLAHFSLIT

#9 AERMPEICTND

Box of Clues

Stumped? Maybe you can find a clue below.

-Apply vapor to exterminate
-Develop
-Portable illuminator
-Ho-_____
-Difficult situation
-Type of auditorium
-List of current assets
-Flourish
-Try
-Sweet material

Arrange the circled letters to solve the mystery answer.

MYSTERY ANSWER ◯◯◯◯◯◯◯◯◯◯◯◯◯◯

MATH

JUMBLE BrainBusters™

Unscramble the Jumbles,
one letter to each square, so
that each equation is correct.

For example:

NONTEOEOW

ONE + ONE = TWO

#1 FWROOTOTUW

◯ ◯ ÷ = ◯

#2 THSITOEEWRX

÷ ◯◯ = ◯

#3 GENEOEINHTIN

◯ − ◯ = ◯

#4 VNIOENESEHTEG

+ ◯ = ◯◯

Then arrange the
circled letters to solve
the mystery equation.

MYSTERY EQUATION

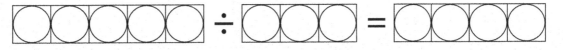

CARNIVORES

JUMBLE BrainBusters™

Unscramble the Jumbles, one letter to each square, to spell names of carnivores.

#1 NLIO

#2 EIGTR

#3 AEYNH

#4 LKCJAA

#5 BERADG

#6 ADPRLOE

Carnivores

Carnivore is the term commonly applied to any animal whose diet consists wholly or largely of meat.

Over time, many carnivores have adapted to an omnivorous diet.

Arrange the circled letters to solve the mystery answer.

MYSTERY ANSWER

JUMBLE CONNECTIONS

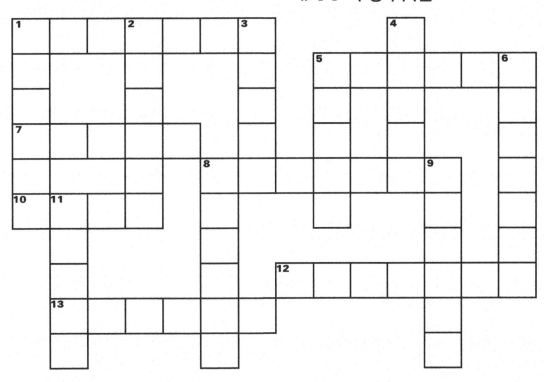

Unscramble the Jumbles, one letter to each square, to spell words that fit into the puzzle below.

ACROSS

- #1 ELTUETC
- #5 HBIGTL
- #7 UAMKC
- #8 ACMALNA
- #10 MUDP
- #12 GPSLIEM
- #13 EGGIDN

DOWN

- #1 ZALDIR
- #2 UETACP
- #3 EELCX
- #4 VLAIL
- #5 RIRBA
- #6 TZAEPRE
- #8 YANOEN
- #9 CUPEOL
- #11 TUTRE

MEANS THE SAME

Unscramble the Jumbles, one letter
to each square, to spell pairs of words
that have the same or similar meanings.

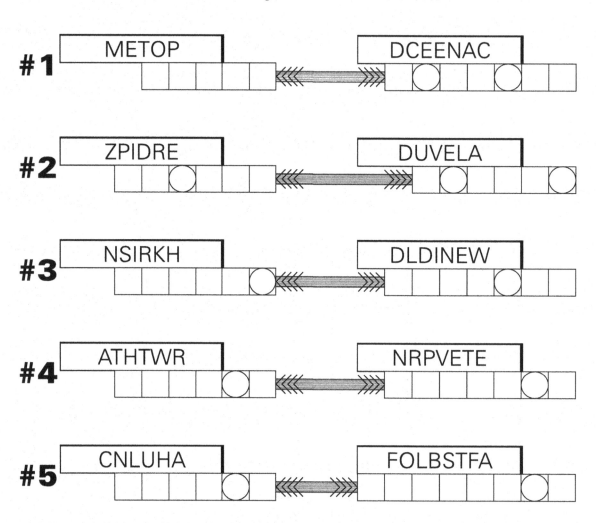

#1 METOP — DCEENAC

#2 ZPIDRE — DUVELA

#3 NSIRKH — DLDINEW

#4 ATHTWR — NRPVETE

#5 CNLUHA — FOLBSTFA

Arrange the circled letters to solve the mystery answer.

MYSTERY ANSWER

ANIMALS

Unscramble the Jumbles, one letter to each square, to spell names of animals.

#1 PHIOP

#2 TLHOS

#3 AMLAL

#4 RUWASL

#5 AFGIERF

#6 AKURTMS

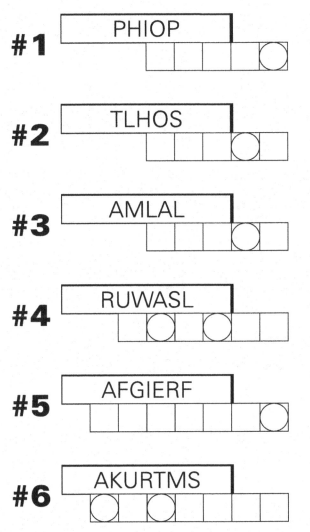

Arrange the circled letters to solve the mystery answer.

Interesting Animal Facts

Giraffes usually sleep standing up.

A mole can dig a tunnel 300 feet long in one night.

Invertebrates are animals that don't have a backbone. Of every 100 animal species, 98 are invertebrates.

MYSTERY ANSWER

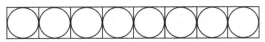

FIND THE JUMBLES®

Unscramble the Jumbles, one letter to each square, to spell words.

#1 ERESCS

#2 LROENL

#3 NJUORI

#4 EDGERE

#5 CSMPAU

#6 ASLCHRO

#7 MACYADE

#8 ARATGDUE

Find and circle the answers (from above) in the grid of letters below.

```
G P R O C Y N V B D R E T U S L
R F N B L A H O L I H L T D C S
A D S G B H M P D E G R E E H P
D U S R E C V P U P O K L J O H
U E S R X C H P U I K H G F L O
A F E N R O L L N S P R U S A O
T V C N Y E A U X O H I O R R L
E E E R O G J W N Y V O P R O P
F D R D Z A C A D E M Y T U O T
```

BIRDS

Unscramble the Jumbles, one letter to each square, to spell varieties of birds.

#1 GEAEL

#2 SROTK

#3 NEPINUG

#4 UBAZDRZ

#5 KEPCAOC

#6 ASRPWRO

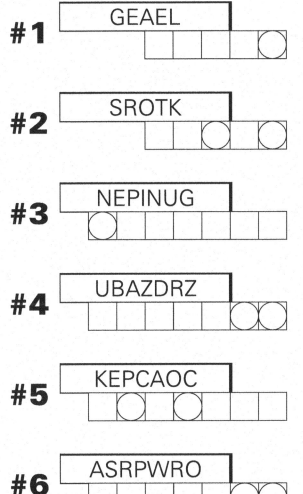

Interesting Bird Facts

Bald eagles build the biggest nests of any bird. Some have measured 10 feet across.

Studies have found that most ducks lay their eggs in the morning.

Penguins have solid bones, unlike most birds, which have hollow bones.

Arrange the circled letters to solve the mystery answer.

MYSTERY ANSWER

WARS AND THE MILITARY

Unscramble the Jumbles, one letter to each square, to spell words related to wars and the military.

#1 KMEUTS

#2 SMIOINS

#3 RAMILDA

#4 HSWRPIA

#5 SIVNAINO

#6 ASOGRINR

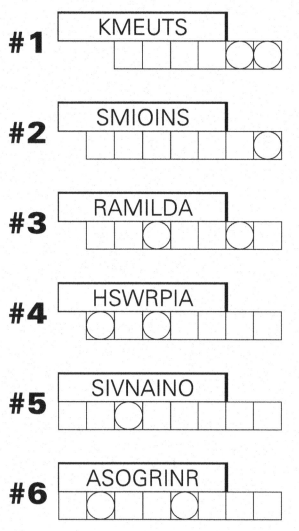

Interesting Military Facts

Because of its use as a staple food by the U.S. Navy, the white bean was christened the "navy bean."

Actor Jimmy Stewart attained the rank of brigadier general in the U.S. Air Force Reserve, the highest U.S. military rank in history for an entertainer.

Arrange the circled letters to solve the mystery answer.

MYSTERY ANSWER

PLANET EARTH

Unscramble the Jumbles, one letter to each square, to spell words related to planet Earth.

#1 SYSAB

#2 HLGUC

#3 LGEOB

#4 SASRG

#5 AIMLCTE

#6 PALAEUT

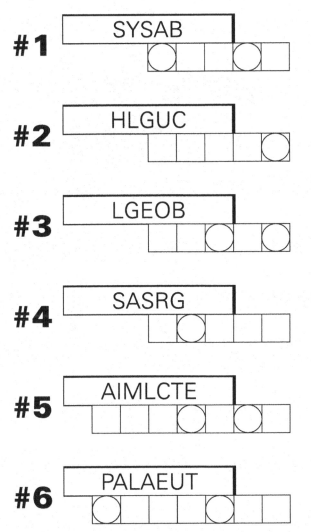

Interesting Planet Earth Facts

The Agulhas current, in the western Indian Ocean, is the fastest ocean current in the world.

There are about 50 geyser fields known to exist on Earth.

There are 91 mountain peaks above 14,000 feet in the United States.

Arrange the circled letters to solve the mystery answer.

MYSTERY ANSWER

puzzle
112

STARTS WITH AND ENDS WITH A VOWEL

JUMBLE
BrainBusters™

Unscramble the Jumbles, one letter to each square, to spell words that start with and end with a vowel.

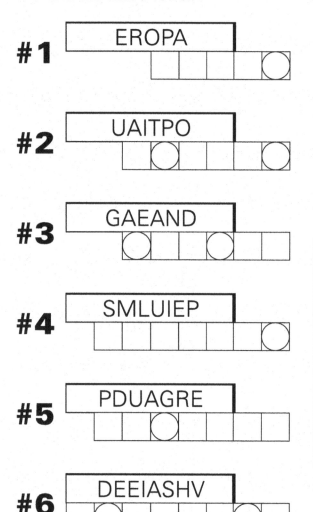

#1 EROPA

#2 UAITPO

#3 GAEAND

#4 SMLUIEP

#5 PDUAGRE

#6 DEEIASHV

Box of Clues

Stumped? Maybe you can find a clue below.

- Place of ideal perfection
- Docket
- _____ house
- Superiority of position
- Spontaneous inclination
- Glue, for example
- Improve

Arrange the circled letters to solve the mystery answer.

MYSTERY ANSWER

114

ALL ABOUT MUSIC

Unscramble the Jumbles, one letter to each square, to spell words related to music.

#1 NAPIO

#2 LOPAK

#3 EOAPR

#4 DROHC

#5 UGIRTA

#6 OTECRCN

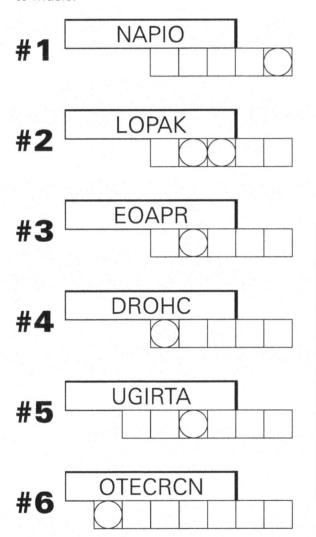

Box of Clues

Stumped? Maybe you can find a clue below.

-Starts with *C*; ends with *D*
-Starts with *P*; ends with *O*
-Starts with *C*; ends with *T*
-Starts with *G*; ends with *R*
-Starts with *P*; ends with *A*
-Starts with *P*; ends with *O*
-Starts with *O*; ends with *A*

Arrange the circled letters to solve the mystery answer.

MYSTERY ANSWER

RHYMES WITH . . .

Unscramble the Jumbles, one letter
to each square, to spell words that will
each have a corresponding rhyming clue.

#1 JGULNE

#2 EMLOLW

#3 CTRITRE

#4 VHANRIS

#5 AGIZRDZ

#6 DUCASTR

#7 AUVLETD

Arrange the circled letters
to solve the mystery answer.

GO · · · NO
TON · · · FUN
BACK · · · STACK
STUCK · · · TRUCK
MISTER · · · SISTER
SCANDAL · · · SANDAL

Box of Clues

Stumped? Maybe you can find a clue
below.

-Rhymes with *yellow*
-Rhymes with *lizard*
-Rhymes with *abundant*
-Rhymes with *salted*
-Rhymes with *bungle*
-Rhymes with *mustard*
-Rhymes with *bitter*
-Rhymes with *tarnish*

MYSTERY ANSWER

MEANS THE OPPOSITE

JUMBLE BrainBusters™

Unscramble the Jumbles, one letter to each square, to spell pairs of words that have opposite or nearly opposite meanings.

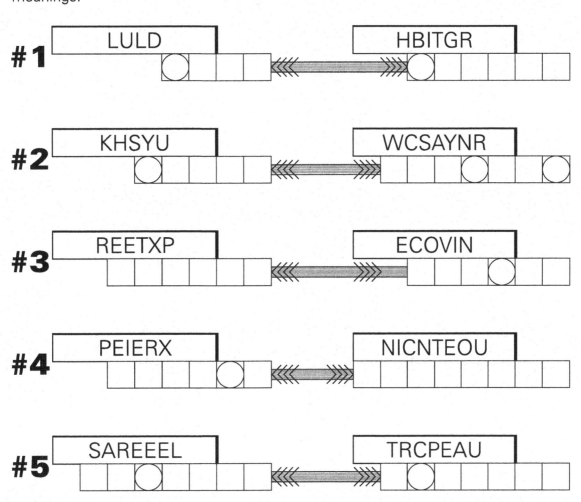

#1 LULD — HBITGR

#2 KHSYU — WCSAYNR

#3 REETXP — ECOVIN

#4 PEIERX — NICNTEOU

#5 SAREEEL — TRCPEAU

Arrange the circled letters to solve the mystery answer.

MYSTERY ANSWER

FIND THE JUMBLES®

Unscramble the Jumbles, one letter
to each square, to spell words.

#1 SYTRO

#2 PORFO

#3 EVYRIF

#4 BEYLIN

#5 CRANHO

#6 LDHIEANE

#7 RERTERPO

#8 NCEWASTS

Find and circle the answers (from above) in the grid of letters below.

```
V H E A D L I N E Z A R T Y O X
A B O Y Y O T T I E U E O R T Z
O R Z D D S S H P Y I T Z O I S
X Y K U D A D E O U P R I T R Y
R C D X C A N C H O R O X S P F
Z I F S I I D T G A L P E O A I
F T W E L P H Z R Y P E J Y P R
D E D Y U X G F S F R R Z O O E
N A B H N I P R O O F D C D R V
```

NINE-LETTER WORDS

Unscramble the Jumbles, one letter
to each square, to spell nine-letter words.

#1 ETAELIATR

#2 MUIHLIAET

#3 GBRAEAELE

#4 ECTASLARO

#5 AORMZHNIE

#6 DANNOEBDA

CONCERNED
DASHBOARD
PUNCTUATE
SAXOPHONE
MOUTHWASH

Box of Clues

Stumped? Maybe you can find a clue
below.

-Demean
-Type of people mover
-Conform, correspond
-Left
-British fortress
-Pleasant
-Even the score

Arrange the circled letters
to solve the mystery answer.

MYSTERY ANSWER

OUTER SPACE

Unscramble the Jumbles, one letter to each square, to spell words related to outer space.

#1 BOITR

#2 CTMEO

#3 ANPTLE

#4 TSUNAR

#5 RUUSNA

#6 SEELIPC

#7 TPENNUE

#8 CEMRYRU

Arrange the circled letters to solve the mystery answer.

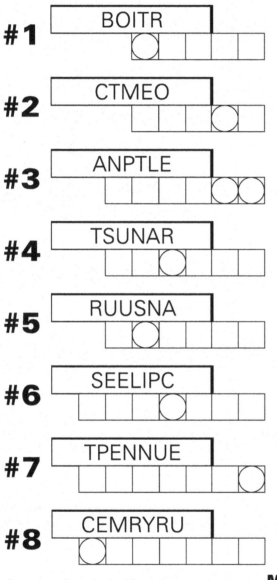

Box of Clues

Stumped? Maybe you can find a clue below.

-Starts with *U*; ends with *S*
-Starts with *C*; ends with *T*
-Starts with *S*; ends with *N*
-Starts with *O*; ends with *T*
-Starts with *M*; ends with *Y*
-Starts with *M*; ends with *E*
-Starts with *P*; ends with *T*
-Starts with *N*; ends with *E*
-Starts with *E*; ends with *E*

MYSTERY ANSWER

BASEBALL TEAMS

Unscramble the Jumbles, one letter to each square, to spell names of Major League baseball teams.

#1 TGSNIA

#2 ARSOLY

#3 SIDINAN

#4 OSCKIRE

#5 AENKESY

#6 GDSODRE

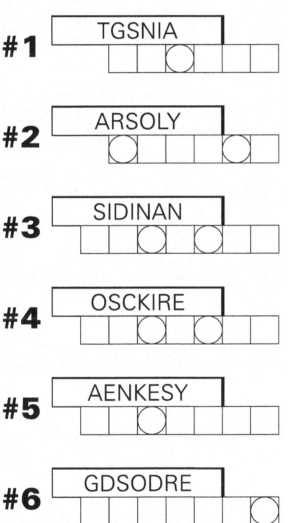

Interesting Baseball Facts

The Houston Astros were originally called the Colt .45s.

Pinstripes were added to New York Yankees jerseys in 1912, only to be shelved for the two following seasons. They were reintroduced in 1915.

Arrange the circled letters to solve the mystery answer.

MYSTERY ANSWER

120

THE BEVERLY HILLBILLIES

Unscramble the Jumbles, one letter to each square, to spell words related to the television show *The Beverly Hillbillies*.

#1 UOCINS

#2 ONBIED

#3 SIMNONA

#4 EWORIWD

#5 BENIHGRO

#6 ARDSLYED

Arrange the circled letters to solve the mystery answer.

Box of Clues

Stumped? Maybe you can find a clue below.

-Jethro, to Elly May
-Milburn _____
-What Jed Clampett was
-Type of home
-*The Beverly Hillbillies* star
-Jethro _____
-Milburn, to Jed and the family

MYSTERY ANSWER

122

JUMBLE®

BrainBusters™

Advanced Puzzles

JUMBLE TRIVIA

Unscramble the Jumbles, one letter to each square, to spell words as suggested by the trivia clues.

#1 Steve _____ is an accomplished banjo player.

TAINRM

#2 Kevin _____ was born on January 18, 1955, in Lynwood, California.

ETCONRS

#3 There are no lakes on this island.

MEUBARD

#4 The ringgit is the official currency of this country.

LAAMSIAY

#5 This explorer died in 1521.

GELANALM

Arrange the circled letters to solve the mystery answer.

The _____ alphabet contains more than 70 letters.

MYSTERY ANSWER

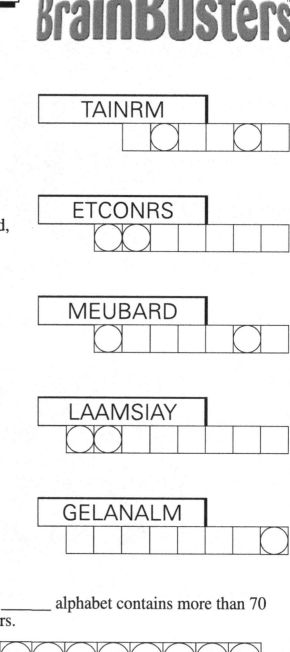

JUMBLE CONNECTIONS

JUMBLE BrainBusters™

Unscramble the Jumbles, one letter to each square, to spell words that fit into the puzzle below.

ACROSS

- **#1** TFLTEUR
- **#5** EWHATL
- **#7** YNEDE
- **#8** MHINELE
- **#10** OYAG
- **#12** TSILKLE
- **#13** PENEHW

DOWN

- **#1** RFENYZ
- **#2** NTUADR
- **#3** ERUEV
- **#4** ANKWE
- **#5** WDRLO
- **#6** AHTHCET
- **#8** AHEENV
- **#9** LEMOYP
- **#11** EZONO

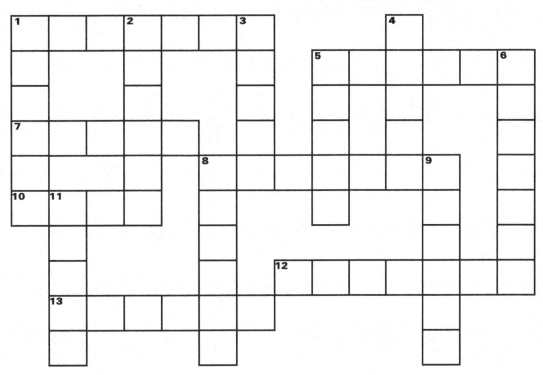

JUMBLE RIDDLES

Unscramble the mixed up letters to
reveal the punch lines to the riddles.

#1 What holds the moon up?

OMONEABMS

#2 What do you call a ship for
good writers?

EPNIMPNSAH

#3 What kind of jokes did
Einstein make?

SWCEACIRKS

#4 What does a dog get when
it graduates from dog
school?

EPDEAIEGR

#5 What two words have
thousands of letters in
them?

FOSPFTOICE

#6 What is a stupid ant?

GNIORNTA

126

ADJECTIVES

Unscramble the Jumbles, one letter
to each square, to spell adjectives.

#1 IGRID

#2 DYITR

#3 HUPSY

#4 RTIYCK

#5 EFEBEL

#6 UEIODVS

#7 HISDOUE

Arrange the circled letters
to solve the mystery answer.

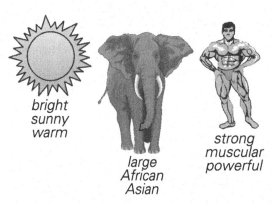

bright
sunny
warm

large
African
Asian

strong
muscular
powerful

Box of Clues

Stumped? Maybe you can find a clue
below.

-Overly aggressive
-Deceptive, cunning
-Weak
-Offensive to the senses
-Difficult
-Absurd
-Filthy
-Strict

MYSTERY ANSWER

JUMBLE CONNECTIONS

Unscramble the Jumbles, one letter to each square, to spell words that fit into the puzzle below.

ACROSS
- #1 AVINEJL
- #5 ETLVEV
- #7 KLOLN
- #8 MDAYNIC
- #10 DTUH
- #12 SEPDIOE
- #13 ERVETR

DOWN
- #1 TUNJKE
- #2 YELIED
- #3 NTTAY
- #4 AIBIL
- #5 VILTA
- #6 TBRELME
- #8 DERVTI
- #9 CREHMO
- #11 RHAYI

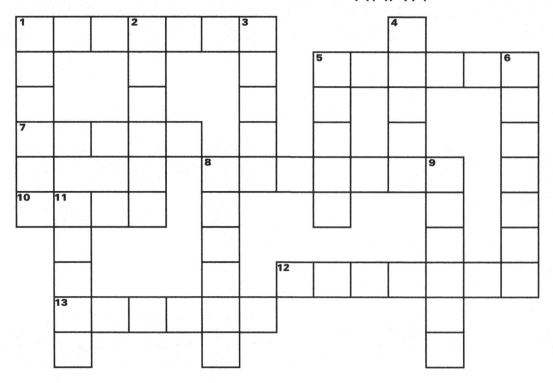

FISHING

JUMBLE BrainBusters™

Unscramble the Jumbles, one letter to each square, to spell words related to fishing.

#1 ITBA

#2 ROMW

#3 EIRVR

#4 TWREA

#5 MIRTPE

#6 BEBORB

#7 NMIWNO

Arrange the circled letters to solve the mystery answer.

Interesting Fishing Facts

Spain has one of the largest fishing fleets in the world.

Longlining is a type of commercial fishing in which thousands of baited hooks are attached to a line that can be miles long.

MYSTERY ANSWER

JUMBLE® TRIVIA

JUMBLE BrainBusters™

Unscramble the Jumbles, one letter to each square, to spell words as suggested by the trivia clues.

#1 One thousand to ten thousand tons of _____ dust fall to Earth each day.

ETREMO

#2 This lies approximately 570 miles southeast of Cape Hatteras, North Carolina.

DMAERUB

#3 There are more than 40,000 characters in _____ script.

SHEECIN

#4 In 1973, New Yorkers spent approximately $100 million buying these.

FRWSELO

#5 This country is composed of four provinces: Balochistan, North-West Frontier Province, Punjab, and Sindh.

AKNPITAS

Arrange the circled letters to solve the mystery answer.

This consists principally of a mixture of hydrocarbons, with traces of various nitrogenous and sulfurous compounds.

MYSTERY ANSWER

FIND THE JUMBLES®

Unscramble the Jumbles, one letter to each square, to spell words.

#1 YPATR

#2 OFORL

#3 EOHSU

#4 ASENET

#5 TELCEDE

#6 EASPKRE

#7 RMINITOY

#8 AMOYRIJT

Find and circle the answers (from above) in the grid of letters below.

```
H S P E A K E R U I P T O P R P
Y K P R C S R M A J O R I T Y U
T R V N K R E L R O S H Y H D O
I G R U O N H O U S E F R U E P
R H R B V R O U O J N N L T T O
O H Y U J L T J B V A X R Y C L
N H J I F B H K E T T U H D E U
I P U P A R T Y T W E R R O L I
M U N R U U P U T P G H K P E P
```

SPORTS

JUMBLE BrainBusters™

Unscramble the Jumbles, one letter to each square, to spell words related to sports.

#1 EHMOR

#2 LEGAIO

#3 DTAFEE

#4 NOSASE

#5 RYIOTCV

#6 ARAENGM

Interesting Sports Facts

A pro volleyball player can spike a volleyball at speeds up to 80 miles per hour.

Crowds of more than 15,000 are common at major badminton tournaments in Malaysia.

Arrange the circled letters to solve the mystery answer.

MYSTERY ANSWER

U.S. STATE CAPITALS

JUMBLE BrainBusters™

Unscramble the Jumbles, one letter to each square, to spell names of U.S. state capitals.

#1 RPREIE

#2 EOKTAP

#3 NSOTOB

#4 LAMOIPY

#5 RODCNOC

#6 UOHLOLNU

Box of Clues

Stumped? Maybe you can find a clue below. (No clue for the mystery answer.)

- Starts with *T*; ends with *A*
- Starts with *C*; ends with *D*
- Starts with *P*; ends with *E*
- Starts with *H*; ends with *U*
- Starts with *O*; ends with *A*
- Starts with *B*; ends with *N*

Arrange the circled letters to solve the mystery answer.

MYSTERY ANSWER

FASHION & CLOTHING

JUMBLE BrainBusters™

Unscramble the Jumbles, one letter to each square, to spell words related to fashion and clothing.

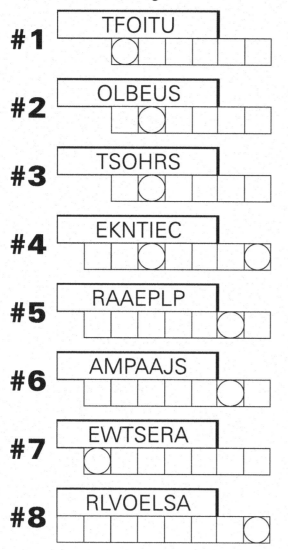

#1 TFOITU

#2 OLBEUS

#3 TSOHRS

#4 EKNTIEC

#5 RAAEPLP

#6 AMPAAJS

#7 EWTSERA

#8 RLVOELSA

Arrange the circled letters to solve the mystery answer.

Interesting Clothing Facts

Michael Jordan has his shirts tailored to fit his 17½-inch neck, 40-inch sleeve, and 39½-inch shirttail.

Almost 50 percent of Americans own at least one piece of clothing with a professional sports team's logo on it.

MYSTERY ANSWER

puzzle 132

FIND THE JUMBLES

Unscramble the Jumbles, one letter to each square, to spell words.

JUMBLE. BrainBusters™

#1 TZOAP

#2 MRBAE

#3 TPYRIE

#4 OIRCZN

#5 UAZRTQ

#6 ARYCSTL

#7 LEMREAD

#8 OIADNDM

Find and circle the answers (from above) in the grid of letters below.

```
O F H G H J K U P U L H P L L K
C H B R D I A M O N D O N E O L
R U T U I L N O L B T U J N P D
Y P O J U K F V U E P Z L O N L
S H P U N G E E T Y T P F K L A
T P A M B E R I F R R I C T O R
A N Z O I O R T A R P H O P B E
L R U P U Y H U I U N Y P P H M
F U I R P U Q P Z I R C O N I E
```

BASEBALL

Unscramble the Jumbles, one letter to each square, to spell words related to baseball.

#1 NCEBH

#2 LVGOE

#3 SEOFNFE

#4 VEAGAER

#5 PSITONIO

#6 FUTOIEDL

JUMBLE® Trivia Quick Quiz

Who would you have been talking to if you had talked to the legendary sportscaster who handled the commentary for the first televised baseball game in 1939?

REREABRDB

ANSWER:

Arrange the circled letters to solve the mystery answer.

MYSTERY ANSWER

JUMBLE CONNECTIONS

Unscramble the Jumbles, one letter to each square, to spell words that fit into the puzzle below.

ACROSS
- #1 TCOLNOR
- #5 LCEOKT
- #7 EWHIG
- #8 CPAGKAE
- #10 UOTB
- #12 CAFLUTY
- #13 ERBOYM

DOWN
- #1 EOBCWB
- #2 TUTGAH
- #3 LAAML
- #4 NICIG
- #5 LKUYC
- #6 RTEIRYF
- #8 APAYPA
- #9 EPYLOM
- #11 RDORE

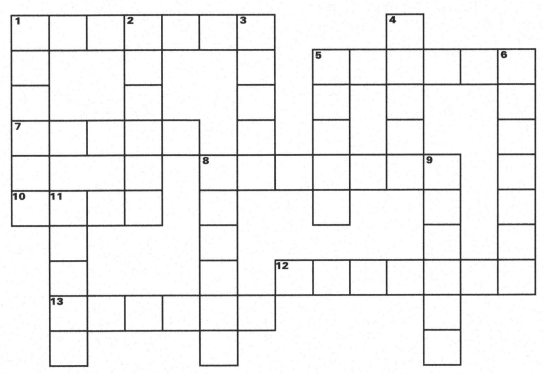

RHYMES WITH . . .

JUMBLE BrainBusters™

Unscramble the Jumbles, one letter to each square, to spell words that will each have a corresponding rhyming clue.

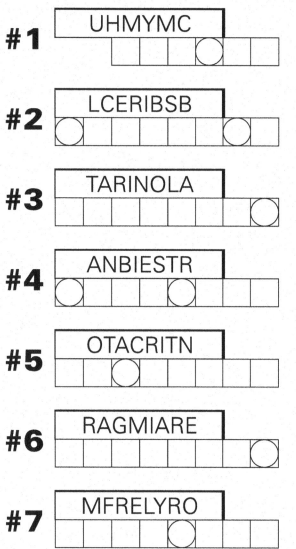

#1 UHMYMC

#2 LCERIBSB

#3 TARINOLA

#4 ANBIESTR

#5 OTACRITN

#6 RAGMIARE

#7 MFRELYRO

GO - - - NO
TON - - - FUN
BACK - - - STACK
STUCK - - - TRUCK
MISTER - - - SISTER
SCANDAL - - - SANDAL

Box of Clues

Stumped? Maybe you can find a clue below.

- Rhymes with *national*
- Rhymes with *fraction*
- Rhymes with *nameless*
- Rhymes with *dummy*
- Rhymes with *nibble*
- Rhymes with *carriage*
- Rhymes with *canister*
- Rhymes with *normally*

Arrange the circled letters to solve the mystery answer.

MYSTERY ANSWER

SUPER JUMBLE® CHALLENGE

JUMBLE BrainBusters™

#1 INW

Unscramble the Jumbles, one letter to each square, to spell words.

#2 KICP

#3 MEYPT

#4 GACFIN

#5 ABLFOIC

#6 OVLITCYE

#7 NEDOESEBL

#8 RCERTSEOPT

#9 AMOMECUINTC

Box of Clues

Stumped? Maybe you can find a clue below.

-Meditation on past events
-A reason to grab a tissue
-Lining at the edge
-Having two focal lengths
-Victory
-Transmit information
-Escape _____
-Choose
-Vacant
-Payment

Arrange the circled letters to solve the mystery answer.

MYSTERY ANSWER

JUMBLE® TRIVIA

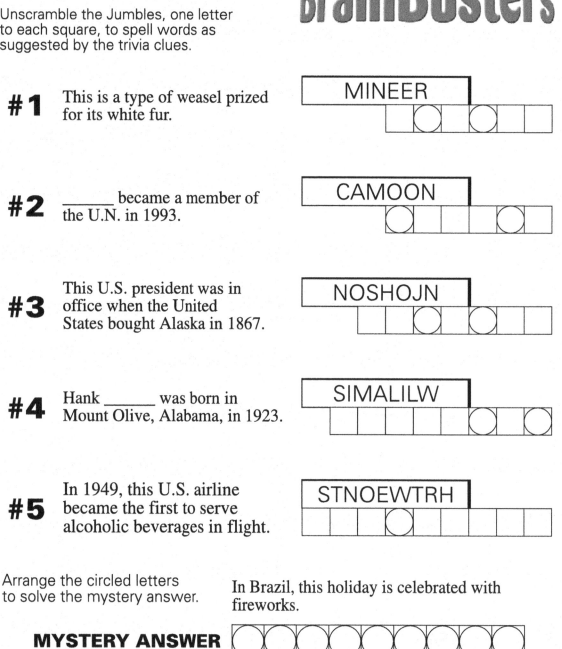

Unscramble the Jumbles, one letter to each square, to spell words as suggested by the trivia clues.

#1 This is a type of weasel prized for its white fur.

MINEER

#2 _____ became a member of the U.N. in 1993.

CAMOON

#3 This U.S. president was in office when the United States bought Alaska in 1867.

NOSHOJN

#4 Hank _____ was born in Mount Olive, Alabama, in 1923.

SIMALILW

#5 In 1949, this U.S. airline became the first to serve alcoholic beverages in flight.

STNOEWTRH

Arrange the circled letters to solve the mystery answer.

In Brazil, this holiday is celebrated with fireworks.

MYSTERY ANSWER

puzzle
138

ALL ABOUT FOOD

JUMBLE BrainBusters

Unscramble the Jumbles, one letter to each square, to spell words related to food.

#1 GSRUA

#2 AIRVOIL

#3 ZTERLPE

#4 TAUSDCR

#5 SLOAHUG

#6 DESOAOF

#7 MTALEOA

Interesting Food Facts

Honey does not spoil.

Fortune cookies were invented in America, in 1918, by Charles Jung.

It takes about one pound of wheat to make three cups of flour.

Arrange the circled letters to solve the mystery answer.

MYSTERY ANSWER

141

STARTS AND ENDS WITH THE SAME LETTER

Unscramble the Jumbles, one letter to each square, to spell words that start and end with the same letter.

#1 RIREV

#2 NEUES

#3 ZRARO

#4 EYLARY

#5 LTLETAS

#6 TGTNIOH

Arrange the circled letters to solve the mystery answer.

JUMBLE BrainBusters™

RADAR
ARENA POP GOING
RIVER HIGH
DICED CRYPTIC

Box of Clues

Stumped? Maybe you can find a clue below. (No clue for the mystery answer.)

-Highest
-*The _____ Show*
-Annually
-Safety _____
-Follow
-The East _____

MYSTERY ANSWER

ALL ABOUT MUSIC

JUMBLE
BrainBusters™

Unscramble the Jumbles, one letter
to each square, to spell words related
to music.

#1 RUSDM

#2 OINILV

#3 NFLEIA

#4 GLTOAE

#5 HMHYRT

#6 ACTATAN

Interesting
Music Facts

The original title of Leonard
Bernstein's musical *West Side
Story* was *East Side Story*.

Irving Berlin never learned to
read or write music.

Arrange the circled letters
to solve the mystery answer.

MYSTERY ANSWER

THE NAME GAME

Unscramble the Jumbles, one letter to each square, to spell last names, as suggested by the first name clues.

Holly _____, born in 1958

#1 THUERN

Sydney _____, born in 1934

#6 CPLKLOA

Peter _____, born in 1950

#2 TRFAPNMO

Joyce _____, born in 1928

#7 OHBERSTR

Richard _____, born in 1941

#3 DEGRHATP

Michael _____, born in 1944

#8 DUSOALG

Kim _____, born in 1953

#4 SEBNGIRA

Tom _____, born in 1940

#9 KBAWOR

Katie _____, born in 1957

#5 RIOCUC

David _____, born in 1947

#10 WBIEO

WEATHER

Unscramble the Jumbles, one letter to each square, to spell words related to weather.

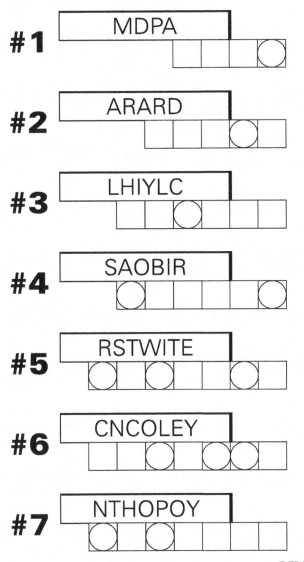

#1 MDPA

#2 ARARD

#3 LHIYLC

#4 SAOBIR

#5 RSTWITE

#6 CNCOLEY

#7 NTHOPOY

Arrange the circled letters to solve the mystery answer.

Interesting Weather Facts

A lightning bolt can generate temperatures hotter than the temperatures found on the sun.

According to NASA, the United States has the world's most violent weather. In a typical year, the United States can expect some 10,000 violent thunderstorms, 5,000 floods, 1,000 tornadoes, and several hurricanes.

MYSTERY ANSWER

JUMBLE CONNECTIONS

Unscramble the Jumbles, one letter to each square, to spell words that fit into the puzzle below.

ACROSS

- #1 SDIUTPE
- #5 ESMCEH
- #7 HRISI
- #8 ATUPNIE
- #10 MIGR
- #12 LMEIAEG
- #13 BOJTCE

DOWN

- #1 UDNRIG
- #2 PSOSMU
- #3 EIERE
- #4 KAIHK
- #5 XIOSU
- #6 BEMAREC
- #8 YCLIOP
- #9 TATCAK
- #11 ROIRG

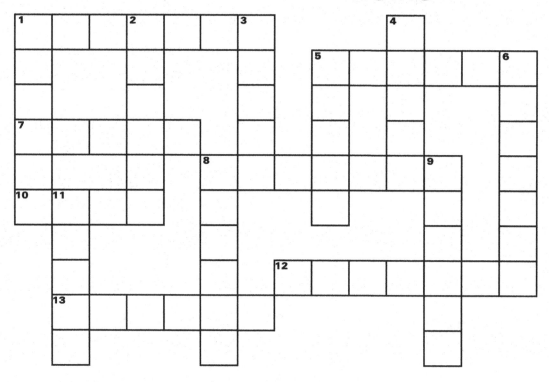

10-LETTER WORDS

JUMBLE BrainBusters™

Unscramble the Jumbles, one letter
to each square, to spell 10-letter words.

#1 DEBELIRAET

#2 GVEEITATNO

#3 FTURADULEN

#4 EPEERMIXTN

#5 RHORESONDU

#6 AUMEORMNMD

APPRENTICE
BRICKLAYER
MANICURIST
PEDESTRIAN
SMOKESTACK

Box of Clues

Stumped? Maybe you can find
a clue below.

-Plant growth
-Dreadful
-Type of note
-Asian country
-Intentional
-Deceitful
-Probe, research

Arrange the circled letters
to solve the mystery answer.

MYSTERY ANSWER

JUMBLE® TRIVIA

JUMBLE.
BrainBusters™

Unscramble the Jumbles, one letter
to each square, to spell words as
suggested by the trivia clues.

#1 _____ belongs to the same
family of plants as
buckwheat.

BAURRBH

#2 The bark of this tree is
fireproof.

DREOOWD

#3 The highest point in _____
is 345 feet above sea level.

DORFAIL

#4 This word is derived from the
French word for "shoe."

GABOSATE

#5 This animal comes in African
and Asian varieties.

NPLEATEH

Arrange the circled
letters to solve the
mystery answer.

This political leader received offers from two NFL
teams but chose instead to take a position as boxing
coach and assistant varsity football coach at Yale.

MYSTERY ANSWER

SUPER JUMBLE® CHALLENGE

#1 YFR

Unscramble the Jumbles, one letter to each square, to spell words.

#2 EZTS

#3 CTIKR

#4 ERLARY

#5 DIWEDNG

#6 URLOEREV

#7 AEMENMUST

#8 MGVNRNTEOE

#9 NAEGIOTOTIN

Box of Clues

Stumped? Maybe you can find a clue below.

- Characteristic peculiarity
- Not often
- _____ park
- Deep-_____
- Serious discussion, talks
- _____ planner
- Gusto
- Ruling authority
- Rule against
- Prank

Arrange the circled letters to solve the mystery answer.

MYSTERY ANSWER

JUMBLE® CONNECTIONS

JUMBLE. BrainBusters™

Unscramble the Jumbles, one letter to each square, to spell words that fit into the puzzle below.

ACROSS

- #1 LBLINIO
- #5 VBHEAE
- #7 ERGOU
- #8 XHAEGNO
- #10 YILW
- #12 EOESRVE
- #13 COCUTL

DOWN

- #1 WBRORO
- #2 RLYUXU
- #3 ECNEI
- #4 IRNHO
- #5 OBAXR
- #6 NCELOES
- #8 CEELKH
- #9 UNASAE
- #11 OIDIT

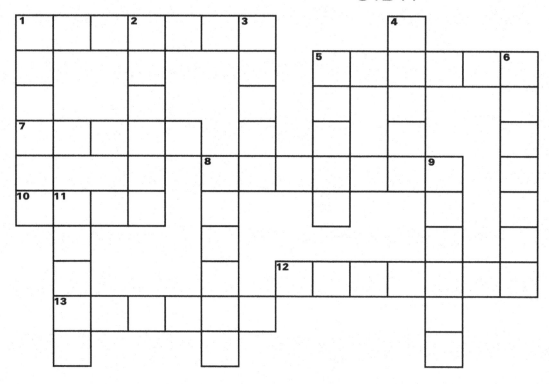

MATH TERMS

Unscramble the Jumbles, one letter to each square, to spell words related to math.

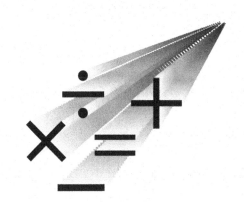

#1 TRIOA

#2 URBMEN

#3 GAERABL

#4 MARLOFU

#5 TINNIYIF

#6 VEISTOIP

Box of Clues

Stumped? Maybe you can find a clue below. (No clue for the mystery answer.)

- Arithmetic that combines letters and numbers
- Proportion
- Natural _____
- Limit of the value of a function or variable when it tends to become numerically larger than any preassigned finite number
- Greater than zero
- Combination of numbers and signs

Arrange the circled letters to solve the mystery answer.

MYSTERY ANSWER

HAWAII

Unscramble the Jumbles, one letter to each square, to spell words related to Hawaii.

#1 GSURA

#2 LHAAO

#3 FAICCIP

#4 GNUFSIR

#5 EHECSBA

#6 NVOAOCL

#7 CPTOILRA

#8 NPIPLEEPA

Arrange the circled letters to solve the mystery answer.

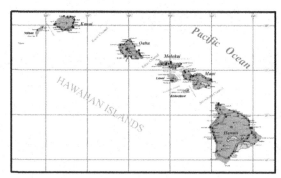

Box of Clues

Stumped? Maybe you can find a clue below. (No clue for the mystery answer.)

-An adjective that describes Hawaii's climate
-Sweet Hawaiian product
-Sea-level recreation areas
-A greeting or farewell
-Hawaiian fruit
-Type of land formation that can be found in Hawaii
-Hawaii's surroundings
-A water activity done in Hawaii

MYSTERY ANSWER

JUMBLE CONNECTIONS

Unscramble the Jumbles, one letter to each square, to spell words that fit into the puzzle below.

ACROSS

#1 AZELUSO
#5 HTACTH
#7 GLUEN
#8 SITMHSU
#10 PYET
#12 HCNIOKO
#13 UCMYMH

DOWN

#1 TAEZLO
#2 ULAGEE
#3 SISWS
#4 ABOYU
#5 GITHT
#6 MHAKOMC
#8 ECONIM
#9 HSOTOM
#11 AYCUC

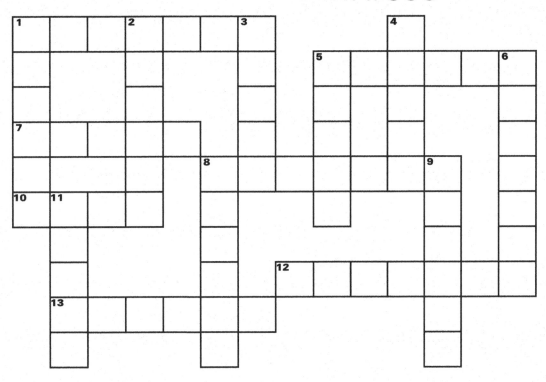

RHYMES WITH . . .

JUMBLE
BrainBusters™

Unscramble the Jumbles, one letter to each square, to spell words that will each have a corresponding rhyming clue.

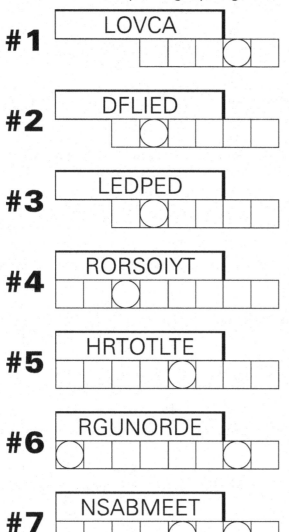

#1 LOVCA

#2 DFLIED

#3 LEDPED

#4 RORSOIYT

#5 HRTOTLTE

#6 RGUNORDE

#7 NSABMEET

GO · · · NO
TON · · · FUN
BACK · · · STACK
STUCK · · · TRUCK
MISTER · · · SISTER
SCANDAL · · · SANDAL

Box of Clues

Stumped? Maybe you can find a clue below.

- Rhymes with *flounder*
- Rhymes with *casement*
- Rhymes with *local*
- Rhymes with *riddle*
- Rhymes with *terminate*
- Rhymes with *bottle*
- Rhymes with *minority*
- Rhymes with *meddle*

Arrange the circled letters to solve the mystery answer.

MYSTERY ANSWER

11-LETTER WORDS

Unscramble the Jumbles, one letter
to each square, to spell 11-letter words.

#1 LINTGELIETN

#2 BFIENYICARE

#3 ZUORNGANEID

#4 SLODPEUAKRE

#5 MCOPRTOLRLE

#6 CKDNOEEAWLG

BELLIGERENT
DESTINATION
HANDWRITING
SPECTACULAR
TRUSTWORTHY

Box of Clues

Stumped? Maybe you can
find a clue below.

- Admit, own
- Smart
- Disjointed
- A device that changes
  electrical signals into
  sounds
- A European country
- Person named to
  receive something
- Type of public auditor

Arrange the circled letters
to solve the mystery answer.

MYSTERY ANSWER

JUMBLE CONNECTIONS

Unscramble the Jumbles, one letter to each square, to spell words that fit into the puzzle below.

ACROSS
- **#1** DANIVLI
- **#5** MATUNU
- **#7** SALAT
- **#8** ROYDREL
- **#10** UDKS
- **#12** LOMLKUS
- **#13** GEGNGO

DOWN
- **#1** NINALD
- **#2** ATAKCT
- **#3** ODNRO
- **#4** SALTL
- **#5** LALYE
- **#6** WNTEKOR
- **#8** RAOROT
- **#9** ROGYUT
- **#11** PEURP

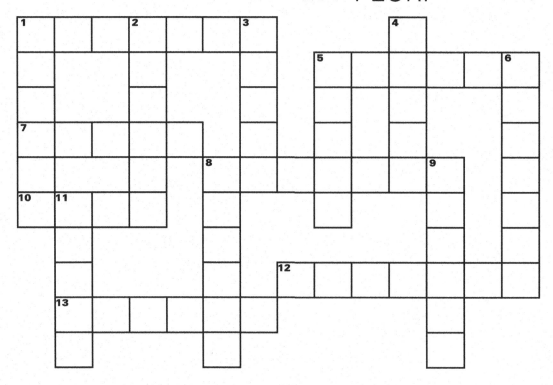

ADJECTIVES

JUMBLE BrainBusters™

Unscramble the Jumbles, one letter to each square, to spell adjectives.

#1 NSYOI

#2 BYLRU

#3 HRBITG

#4 GJGDEA

#5 EISCAPL

#6 CVISOIU

#7 EULJOSA

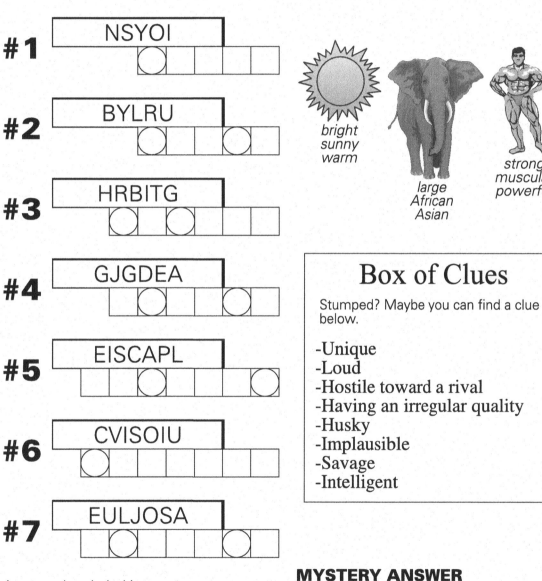

bright sunny warm

large African Asian

strong muscular powerful

Box of Clues

Stumped? Maybe you can find a clue below.

- Unique
- Loud
- Hostile toward a rival
- Having an irregular quality
- Husky
- Implausible
- Savage
- Intelligent

Arrange the circled letters to solve the mystery answer.

MYSTERY ANSWER

SUPER JUMBLE® CHALLENGE

JUMBLE BrainBusters™

#1 LXA

Unscramble the Jumbles, one letter to each square, to spell words.

#2 ANYV

#3 OGRPU

#4 RENTYS

#5 REABRIR

#6 MIWMIGNS

#7 ASAITSTNS

#8 TNAATHMETC

#9 NORATIELIAZ

Box of Clues

Stumped? Maybe you can find a clue below.

- Affection, fondness
- Gathering
- _____ pool
- Explain
- _____ yard
- Helper
- Blockade
- Conservancy
- Loose, slack
- Guard

Arrange the circled letters to solve the mystery answer.

MYSTERY ANSWER ◯◯◯◯◯◯◯◯◯◯◯◯◯◯

puzzle
156

STARTS AND ENDS WITH THE SAME LETTER

JUMBLE BrainBusters™

Unscramble the Jumbles, one letter to each square, to spell words that start and end with the same letter.

#1 AMMDA

#2 EHAHRT

#3 HICTETK

#4 CSUSCES

#5 EGRULRA

#6 DIOADMN

RADAR
ARENA POP GOING
RIVER   HIGH
DICED CRYPTIC

Box of Clues

Stumped? Maybe you can find a clue below. (No clue for the mystery answer.)

-Type of fireproof area
-Favorable outcome
-Dense growth of shrubbery
-Normal
-Lady
-_____ ring

Arrange the circled letters to solve the mystery answer.

MYSTERY ANSWER

JUMBLE CONNECTIONS

Unscramble the Jumbles, one letter to each square, to spell words that fit into the puzzle below.

ACROSS
- #1 JILKYOL
- #5 OVOODO
- #7 WTEDE
- #8 GLNIOGN
- #10 NYEV
- #12 LTESIUN
- #13 YTPTIS

DOWN
- #1 KLETET
- #2 OLNEYL
- #3 HYOAO
- #4 NTOIX
- #5 EREVG
- #6 ATAOMEL
- #8 HLAISV
- #9 SGLOYS
- #11 TNUYT

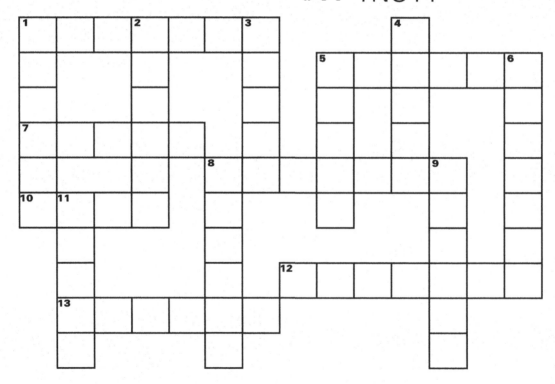

RHYMES WITH . . .

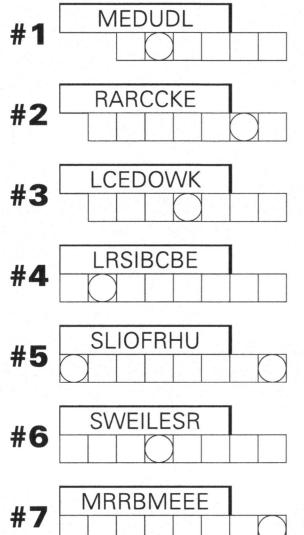

Unscramble the Jumbles, one letter to each square, to spell words that will each have a corresponding rhyming clue.

#1 MEDUDL

#2 RARCCKE

#3 LCEDOWK

#4 LRSIBCBE

#5 SLIOFRHU

#6 SWEILESR

#7 MRRBMEEE

Arrange the circled letters to solve the mystery answer.

JUMBLE BrainBusters™

GO · · · NO
TON · · · FUN
BACK · · · STACK
STUCK · · · TRUCK
MISTER · · · SISTER
SCANDAL · · · SANDAL

Box of Clues

Stumped? Maybe you can find a clue below.

- Rhymes with *tireless*
- Rhymes with *cuddle*
- Rhymes with *December*
- Rhymes with *backer*
- Rhymes with *dribble*
- Rhymes with *fearful*
- Rhymes with *nourish*
- Rhymes with *deadlock*

MYSTERY ANSWER

SUPER JUMBLE® CHALLENGE

JUMBLE BrainBusters™

#1 OMW

Unscramble the Jumbles, one letter to each square, to spell words.

#2 ENTX

#3 SPUYH

Box of Clues

Stumped? Maybe you can find a clue below.

-Manner of conducting oneself
-Surroundings
-Aggressive
-Cut, trim
-Projecting gallery
-_____ office
-Pedigreed animal
-Ensuing
-Fortify
-Capture

#4 BCANRH

#5 LBACNYO

#6 ABEORVIH

#7 DAPEPHENR

#8 SGETNRTHNE

#9 MNVEIROTNEN

Arrange the circled letters to solve the mystery answer.

MYSTERY ANSWER

MEANS THE SAME

Unscramble the Jumbles, one letter
to each square, to spell pairs of words
that have the same or similar meanings.

#1 BSLMOY — MBEEML

#2 RMHITE — CREUELS

#3 CDDUTE — CTAUSRTB

#4 AGPILEL — ELPNRUD

#5 NEEFTRV — UZAEOSL

Arrange the circled letters to solve the mystery answer.

MYSTERY ANSWER

JUMBLE® CONNECTIONS

JUMBLE®
BrainBusters™

Unscramble the Jumbles, one letter to each square, to spell words that fit into the puzzle below.

ACROSS

- #1 NOIMKGD
- #5 PEPRPE
- #7 RCOCU
- #8 EIRHOEN
- #10 ADHN
- #12 PBUHLIS
- #13 LEVTRO

DOWN

- #1 BHKISO
- #2 RGONDU
- #3 MEIVO
- #4 ANORP
- #5 POTIV
- #6 BUSRBIH
- #8 DHULDE
- #9 XEPEIR
- #11 AUERZ

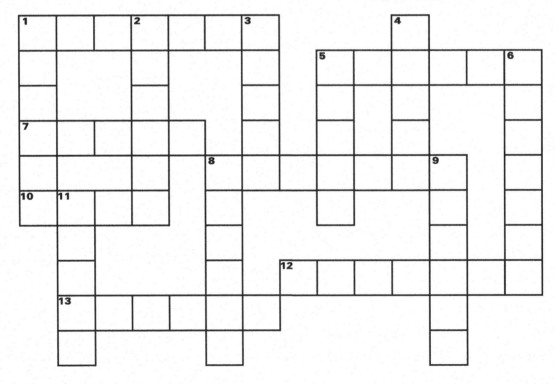

AFRICAN COUNTRIES

JUMBLE BrainBusters™

Unscramble the Jumbles, one letter to each square, to spell names of African countries.

#1 BAYIL

#2 AENKY

#3 RILEBIA

#4 RINEIAG

#5 AELNGSE

#6 RCOMCOO

Box of Clues

Stumped? Maybe you can find a clue below.

-Starts with *N*; ends with *A*
-Starts with *L*; ends with *A*
-Starts with *K*; ends with *A*
-Starts with *M*; ends with *O*
-Starts with *L*; ends with *A*
-Starts with *S*; ends with *A*
-Starts with *S*; ends with *L*

Arrange the circled letters to solve the mystery answer.

MYSTERY ANSWER

FIND THE JUMBLES

Unscramble the Jumbles, one letter to each square, to spell words.

#1 SEIABZL

#2 ESMSIVA

#3 MIEMNES

#4 SCLOSALO

#5 GCGAITIN

#6 SACUPIOS

#7 PMIOINSG

#8 UNOREMOS

Find and circle the answers (from above) in the grid of letters below.

```
G H R D C G S P A C I O U S L E
N F K C E J I L O T V P E K M N
I Z J T B M A G C B N H O N A O
S Y U O U S R D A S E A N B S R
O T P H S N P N L N L O P O S M
P A B O A E O P F O T R W H I O
M T L H P T U T P F U I I M V U
I O S I Z A B L E D E N C O E S
C F D E T I M M E N S E K L P R
```

SUPER JUMBLE® CHALLENGE

JUMBLE
BrainBusters™

Unscramble the Jumbles, one letter
to each square, to spell words.

#1 EJT

#2 CEUT

#3 XTOCI

#4 NREUNR

#5 TARTCTA

#6 SOLCOSLA

#7 CMIFAILSE

#8 PEMSRBMEIH

#9 RHACOPELIAG

Box of Clues

Stumped? Maybe you can find a clue below.

-Reproduction
-_____ card or _____ fees
-Jogger
-_____ engine
-Enormous
-Type of candy
-Adorable
-Group of islands
-Noxious
-Enchant

Arrange the circled
letters to solve the
mystery answer.

MYSTERY ANSWER

12-LETTER WORDS

Unscramble the Jumbles, one letter
to each square, to spell 12-letter words.

#1 NUIRSDICIOJT

#2 BABEIVNRIATO

#3 TAFYTISACSOR

#4 ETSPVERCIELY

#5 HRERCTCTIUEA

#6 NCTOFIMINORA

APPENDECTOMY
CONTEMPORARY
PRACTITIONER
SUBSCRIPTION
DISAGREEABLE
HANDKERCHIEF

Box of Clues

Stumped? Maybe you
can find a clue below.

-In the order given
-Abridgment
-Science of a
 building
-A U.S. city
-Corroboration
-Adequate
-Territory within
 one's authority

Arrange the circled
letters to solve the
mystery answer.

MYSTERY ANSWER

168

RHYMES WITH . . .

Unscramble the Jumbles, one letter to each square, to spell words that will each have a corresponding rhyming clue.

#1 LUEMJB

#2 EAZLUOS

#3 BLRUCME

#4 BRIHTCSE

#5 FUNNIOAT

#6 ESDELSES

#7 SGROACIU

Arrange the circled letters to solve the mystery answer.

JUMBLE BrainBusters™

GO - - - NO
TON - - - FUN
BACK - - - STACK
STUCK - - - TRUCK
MISTER - - - SISTER
SCANDAL - - - SANDAL

Box of Clues

Stumped? Maybe you can find a clue below.

-Rhymes with *grumble*
-Rhymes with *jealous*
-Rhymes with *nauseous*
-Rhymes with *stumble*
-Rhymes with *needless*
-Rhymes with *stitches*
-Rhymes with *spacious*
-Rhymes with *mountain*

MYSTERY ANSWER

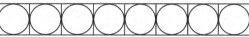

FIND THE JUMBLES

Unscramble the Jumbles, one letter
to each square, to spell words.

#1 TMOHN

#2 ADEDCE

#3 SENOAS

#4 DSCONE

#5 NEOMTM

#6 ANSTINT

#7 UCRENYT

#8 LMIFTEIE

Find and circle the answers (from above) in the grid of letters below.

```
A X F V B O P D T K M L E T W G
H D X Z V I L O E O L O U N E P
F O E T F W H I H C H L N A S C
S K U P U D L P F I A L P T P L
L E H Y N R E N M E K D C S H H
U P A O U M O M E N T P E N P O
U Y C S O H O Y U R S I P I O P
J E H T O J N R P E K O M P I L
S B C C E N T U R Y P F J E U T
```

Bonus
Puzzles

TumbleWords™

From the People Who Bring You JUMBLE®

TumbleWords™

① ___HOWIE___ _____

② _____ _____

③ _____ _____

④ _____ _____

⑤ _____ _____

⑥ _____ _____

⑦ _____ _____

⑧ _____ _____

⑨ _____ _____

⑩ _____ ___LETTER___

*If you
get stumped . . .
work
backward!*

**HOW
TO
PLAY**

Look at the
clue to solve
#1. The second
part of the answer
to #1 is the first part
of the answer to #2
and so on.
Example:

① __TIME__ __OUT__ Sports break time
② __OUT__ __LOUD__ As to be heard
③ __LOUD__ __NOISE__ Reason to cover ears

CLUES

① A football commentator

② Los Angeles area shipping hub

③ Large cloth

④ One way to get dry

⑤ Way from the center

⑥ A basketball term

⑦ Judge's place of business

⑧ Access provider at a hotel

⑨ You might keep this in your pocket

⑩ Correspondence for many

172

From the People Who Bring You JUMBLE®

TumbleWords™

① _____ AT _____ _____

② _____ _____ _____

③ _____ _____ _____

④ _____ _____ _____

⑤ _____ _____ _____

⑥ _____ _____ _____

⑦ _____ _____ _____

⑧ _____ _____ _____

⑨ _____ _____ _____

⑩ _____ _____ FACE _____

If you get stumped . . . work backward!

HOW TO PLAY

Look at the clue to solve #1. The second part of the answer to #1 is the first part of the answer to #2 and so on. Example:

① _TIME_ _OUT_ Sports break time

② _OUT_ _LOUD_ As to be heard

③ _LOUD_ _NOISE_ Reason to cover ears

CLUES

① Finally

② Gates, to Bill

③ ____ ____ Tune

④ Marlo Thomas TV show

⑤ Young female troop member

⑥ Type of group

⑦ Scout manager

⑧ Used to display best scores

⑨ Boxed competition

⑩ Competitive look

From the People Who Bring You JUMBLE®

TumbleWords™

① ____ DR. ____ ____

② ____ ____

③ ____ ____

④ ____ ____

⑤ ____ ____

⑥ ____ ____

⑦ ____ – ____

⑧ ____ ____

⑨ ____ ____

⑩ ____ SUPPLIES

If you get stumped . . . work backward!

HOW TO PLAY

Look at the clue to solve #1. The second part of the answer to #1 is the first part of the answer to #2 and so on. Example:

① TIME   OUT   Sports break time
② OUT   LOUD   As to be heard
③ LOUD   NOISE   Reason to cover ears

CLUES

① 1962 movie

② Bad

③ Enjoyable film

④ Reason to look in the paper

⑤ An NYC landmark

⑥ Beginning shape

⑦ ____-____ street

⑧ One-____ ____

⑨ Where you might buy a seat

⑩ Staplers and paper clips

From the People Who Bring You JUMBLE®

TumbleWords™

① __SOCIAL__ _____

② _____ _____

③ _____ _____

④ _____ _____

⑤ _____ _____

⑥ _____ _____

⑦ _____ _____

⑧ _____ _____

⑨ _____ _____

⑩ _____ __MECHANISM__

*If you
get stumped . . .
work
backward!*

HOW TO PLAY

Look at the clue to solve #1. The second part of the answer to #1 is the first part of the answer to #2 and so on. Example:

① __TIME__ __OUT__ Sports break time

② __OUT__ __LOUD__ As to be heard

③ __LOUD__ __NOISE__ Reason to cover ears

CLUES

① A government program

② Maximum ____ ____

③ Type of escape

④ ____ ____ bank

⑤ *Land of* ____ ____ (TV show)

⑥ *Jurassic Park* sequel

⑦ Major military conflict

⑧ Military conflict area

⑨ A basketball strategy

⑩ Type of unconscious mental process

175

From the People Who Bring You JUMBLE®

TumbleWords™

① __LOOK-__ _____

② _____ _____

③ _____ _____

④ _____ _____

⑤ _____ _____

⑥ _____ _____

⑦ _____ _____

⑧ _____ _____

⑨ _____ _____

⑩ _____ __REEF__

If you get stumped . . . work backward!

HOW TO PLAY

Look at the clue to solve #1. The second part of the answer to #1 is the first part of the answer to #2 and so on. Example:

① __TIME__ __OUT__ Sports break time
② __OUT__ __LOUD__ As to be heard
③ __LOUD__ __NOISE__ Reason to cover ears

CLUES

① General visual survey

② Become angry

③ The International ____ ____

④ Heated exchange of words

⑤ A large vehicle

⑥ Type of roadside business

⑦ Reason to put on the brakes

⑧ A form of communication

⑨ Linguistic blockade

⑩ The Great ____ ____

From the People Who Bring You JUMBLE®

TumbleWords™

① ___TALK___ _____

② _____ _____

③ _____ _____

④ _____ _____

⑤ _____ _____

⑥ _____ _____

⑦ _____ _____

⑧ _____ _____

⑨ _____ _____

⑩ _____ ___WEST___

If you get stumped . . . work backward!

HOW TO PLAY

Look at the clue to solve #1. The second part of the answer to #1 is the first part of the answer to #2 and so on. Example:

① _TIME_ _OUT_ Sports break time

② _OUT_ ↙ _LOUD_ As to be heard

③ _LOUD_ ↙ _NOISE_ Reason to cover ears

CLUES

① Type of TV program

② Actor's profession

③ CNBC's specialty

④ Important bulletin

⑤ One result of heavy rain

⑥ Reason to head for higher ground

⑦ Early indication

⑧ Terminate transmission

⑨ Not in tune

⑩ Florida island

From the People Who Bring You JUMBLE®

TumbleWords™

① ____THE____ _____

② _____ _____

③ _____ _____

④ _____ _____

⑤ _____ _____

⑥ _____ _____

⑦ _____ _____

⑧ _____ _____

⑨ _____ _____

⑩ _____ ____HOME____

If you get stumped . . . work backward!

HOW TO PLAY

Look at the clue to solve #1. The second part of the answer to #1 is the first part of the answer to #2 and so on. Example:

① _TIME_ _OUT_ Sports break time
② _OUT_ _LOUD_ As to be heard
③ _LOUD_ _NOISE_ Reason to cover ears

CLUES

① ____ ____ *News Bears* (movie)

② Unfortunate, untimely situation

③ ____ ____ ice

④ ____ ____ Channel

⑤ Meteorological update

⑥ Type of student review

⑦ A magician's feat

⑧ One-____ ____

⑨ Short trip on a small horse

⑩ "Do you need a ____ ____?"

From the People Who Bring You JUMBLE®

TumbleWords™

If you
get stumped . . .
work
backward!

① ALMOST _____

② _____ _____

③ _____ _____

④ _____ _____

⑤ _____ _____

⑥ _____ _____

⑦ _____ _____

⑧ _____ _____

⑨ _____ _____

⑩ _____ QUARTERS

HOW TO PLAY

Look at the clue to solve #1. The second part of the answer to #1 is the first part of the answer to #2 and so on. Example:

① TIME   OUT   Sports break time
② OUT   LOUD   As to be heard
③ LOUD   NOISE   Reason to cover ears

CLUES

① Nearly as good as it can be

② *The* ____ ____ (movie)

③ Type of weather bulletin

④ Precursor of a problem

⑤ Terminate a transmission

⑥ Not prepared

⑦ Protective canine

⑧ Canine "home"

⑨ Visitor to a home

⑩ Visitor's sleeping area

From the People Who Bring You JUMBLE®

TumbleWords™

① __PRIVATE__ _____

② _____ _____

③ _____ _____

④ _____ _____

⑤ _____ _____

⑥ _____ _____

⑦ _____ _____

⑧ _____ _____

⑨ _____ _____

⑩ _____ __WHEEL__

If you
get stumped . . .
work
backward!

HOW TO PLAY

Look at the clue to solve #1. The second part of the answer to #1 is the first part of the answer to #2 and so on. Example:

① __TIME__ __OUT__ Sports break time
② __OUT__ __LOUD__ As to be heard
③ __LOUD__ __NOISE__ Reason to cover ears

CLUES

① Exclusive association

② A carbonated beverage

③ Coke, for example

④ Surprise exam

⑤ The ____ ____ time

⑥ Standard ____ ____

⑦ Type of document

⑧ Mental strength

⑨ Car director's helper

⑩ Device found on a car

ANSWERS

1. **Jumbles:** #1. WALK #2. HOMER #3. TRIPLE #4. STRIKE #5. ROOKIE #6. DUGOUT
   Mystery Answer: STADIUM

2. **Jumbles:** #1. MONDALE #2. PAULEY #3. ROBERTS #4. ASHCROFT #5. CASSIDY #6. SHRIVER #7. HILFIGER #8. REAGAN #9. JENNINGS #10. TRUMP

3. **Jumbles:** #1. DOVE #2. CROW #3. RAVEN #4. PIGEON #5. CHICKEN #6. VULTURE
   Mystery Answer: PARTRIDGE

4. **Jumbles:** #1. AORTA #2. USAGE #3. UNLIKE #4. ARMADA #5. INCOME #6. IMMERSE
   Mystery Answer: IMMEDIATE

5. **Jumbles:** #1. CHILE #2. THUNDER #3. ECUADOR #4. WYOMING #5. JEFFERSON
   Mystery Answer: GREYHOUND

6. **Jumbles:** #1. LENNY #2. SHOTZ #3. SITCOM #4. CARMINE #5. MARSHALL #6. MILWAUKEE
   Mystery Answer: ROOMMATES

7. **Jumbles:** #1. HAIL #2. FRONT #3. STORM #4. DEGREES #5. RAINFALL #6. FORECAST
   Mystery Answer: FLOODING

8. **Jumbles:** #1. IVORY #2. BLACK #3. MAUVE #4. BROWN #5. VIOLET #6. PURPLE #7. YELLOW #8. LAVENDER

9. **Jumbles:** #1. SIEGE #2. BULLET #3. WEAPON #4. BOMBER #5. GUNFIRE #6. DEFECTOR
   Mystery Answer: AIR FORCE

10. **Jumbles:** #1. LUCID #2. BRAVE #3. HASTY #4. BLEAK #5. LOCAL #6. GLOSSY #7. GRUMPY
    Mystery Answer: HORRIBLE

11. **Jumbles:** #1. GOULASH #2. HOMER #3. MUSTARD #4. A STAMP #5. ON THE DECK #6. IN FINLAND

12. **Jumbles:** #1. OUNCE #2. TICKET #3. POUNDS #4. NUMBER #5. REFEREE #6. DECEMBER
    Mystery Answer: SEPTEMBER

13. **Jumbles:** #1. BOLD #2. BUNNY #3. BABOON #4. BENEFIT #5. BARGAIN #6. BURGLAR #7. BROTHER #8. BALLOON
    Mystery Answer: BLUEBIRD

14. **Jumbles:** #1. HAMMOCK #2. BREEZE #3. CAREFREE #4. DANCE #5. CHILDREN #6. DRIFT #7. IDEAL
    Mystery Answer: RECREATION

15. **Jumbles:** #1A. SUNBURN #5A. BELONG #7A. MOUND #8A. HEIRESS #10A. RASH #12A. MISTAKE #13A. SLOGAN #1D. SUMMER #2D. BRANCH #3D. NUDGE #4D. CLASS #5D. BERRY #6D. GAZELLE #8D. HUBCAP #9D. SAFARI #11D. AMISS

16. **Jumbles:** #1. MAINE #2. NEVADA #3. ARIZONA #4. WYOMING #5. ALABAMA #6. NEBRASKA #7. DELAWARE
    Mystery Answer: MARYLAND

17. **Jumbles:** #1. HILL #2. CREEK #3. ISLAND #4. VALLEY #5. JUNGLE #6. TUNDRA
    Mystery Answer: AVALANCHE

18. **Jumbles:** #1. TYLER #2. SKYLAB #3. ZEALAND #4. SCOTLAND #5. FORT KNOX
    Mystery Answer: BROOKLYN

19. **Jumbles:** #1. TIGHT #2. SERIES #3. NOTION #4. WINDOW #5. MAGNUM #6. TRUMPET
    Mystery Answer: MUSHROOM

20. **Jumbles:** #1. MIGHT #2. RUBBER #3. TOMATO #4. GLACIAL #5. CRUMBLE #6. STAMMER
    Mystery Answer: GRACIOUS

21. **Jumbles:** #1. ONE–ONE=ZERO #2. FOUR–TWO=TWO #3. FIVE+FIVE=TEN #4. SIX+SIX=TWELVE
    Mystery Equation: TWO x TWO = FOUR

22. **Jumbles:** #1. FROG #2. CAMEL #3. LIZARD #4. RABBIT #5. COUGAR #6. MONKEY
    Mystery Answer: CROCODILE

23. **Jumbles:** #1. PAWN #2. MOVE #3. PIECE #4. CHECK #5. BOARD #6. MATCH #7. KNIGHT #8. BISHOP

24. **Jumbles:** #1. ONExONE=ONE #2. SEVEN–FIVE=TWO #3. FOURxTWO=EIGHT #4. FOUR–THREE=ONE
    Mystery Equation: EIGHT + ONE = NINE

25. **Jumbles:** #1A. DISPUTE #5A. THWART #7A. USHER #8A. DECIBEL #10A. EVEN #12A. HABITAT #13A. UNUSED #1D. DELUXE #2D. PIGEON #3D. ENSURE #4D. AWARE #5D. TULIP #6D. TORMENT #8D. DOCKET #9D. LETTER #11D. VALUE

26. **Jumbles:** #1. POODLES #2. A TRIFLE #3. TO THE DOCK #4. RED TAPE #5. GRAVELY #6. A HOLE

27. **Jumbles:** #1. MAINE #2. NEPTUNE #3. GIRAFFE #4. TERMITES #5. BRADSHAW
    Mystery Answer: HUMMINGBIRD

28. **Jumbles:** #1. POUND #2. OUNCE #3. BARREL #4. BUSHEL #5. GALLON #6. MICRON #7. FURLONG #8. TEASPOON

29. **Jumbles:** #1. AGILE #2. BRISK #3. ADRIFT
#4. STRONG #5. FAMOUS #6. LENGTHY
#7. ZEALOUS
Mystery Answer: AMAZING

30. **Jumbles:** #1A. GOGGLES #5A. EXTORT
#7A. SCUBA #8A. PERHAPS #10A. PUNT
#12A. SCOOTER #13A. ONWARD #1D. GOSSIP
#2D. GAMBIT #3D. STYLE #4D. STUMP
#5D. EIGHT #6D. TWISTER #8D. PASTRY
#9D. SENTRY #11D. UNION

31. **Jumbles:** #1. ELOPE #2. YUMMY #3. STATUS
#4. CRYPTIC #5. DISCARD #6. ROOSTER
Mystery Answer: SUPPRESS

32. **Jumbles:** #1. TROUBLE #2. NOTHING #3. A RIVER
#4. A FEATHER #5. IMPORTANT #6. YOUR BREATH

33. **Jumbles:** #1. TWINS #2. TIGERS #3. BRAVES
#4. ORIOLES #5. MARLINS #6. BREWERS
Mystery Answer: MARINERS

34. **Jumbles:** #1. LIMB #2. TRUNK #3. SPRUCE
#4. BRANCH #5. CYPRESS #6. REDWOOD
Mystery Answer: SYCAMORE

35. **Jumbles:** #1. DRY #2. BARK #3. MERCY
#4. FROLIC #5. CENSURE #6. DILIGENT
#7. AVAILABLE #8. ESPECIALLY #9. INDEPENDENT
Mystery Answer: PENNSYLVANIA

36. **Jumbles:** #1. CRAYON #2. DEAD SEA
#3. COOLIDGE #4. STAR TREK #5. COMPUTERS
Mystery Answer: RED CROSS

37. **Jumbles:** #1. COACH #2. TRIPLE #3. BATTER
#4. SEASON #5. DOUBLE #6. SCORING
#7. STADIUM #8. MANAGER

```
T E G H R D S C O R I N G O I S
T H U I O P O R S T U O P R D T
Y R L U L F P U F E D C X N X A
H O I N M B I H B R E T O O P D
B U I P Y V C R B L N I O S B I
F O R N L A T I O R E W N A B U
T R T U O E O P I U P P L E H M
U G N C M A N A G E R N I S N O
H I H B A T T E R O P J K L O L
```

38. **Jumbles:** #1. DRUMS #2. A NITWIT
#3. A TUNA FISH #4. SCREENS #5. A PICCOLO
#6. YOUR LAP

39. **Jumbles:** #1. ONExONE=ONE #2. FIVE+FIVE=TEN
#3. FIVE+TWO=SEVEN #4. TEN+TEN=TWENTY
Mystery Equation: SEVEN + TWO = NINE

40. **Jumbles:** #1. THIRD #2. SNEEZE #3. NUZZLE #4.
MUTTER #5. CRICKET #6. PASSIVE #7. FEATHER
Mystery Answer: SLITHERS

41. **Jumbles:** #1A. DWINDLE #5A. GARAGE #7A. ALIBI
#8A. BLEMISH #10A. MOVE #12A. EARPLUG
#13A. INVEST #1D. DISARM #2D. NIMBLE
#3D. EXPEL #4D. GROSS #5D. GAMMA
#6D. ETCHING #8D. BYPASS #9D. HOLLOW
#11D. OASIS

42. **Jumbles:** #1. TAX #2. HOLD #3. PIANO
#4. JOSTLE #5. MUFFLER #6. FATALITY
#7. OBNOXIOUS #8. CONFERENCE
#9. FINGERPRINT
Mystery Answer: PROFESSIONAL

43. **Jumbles:** #1. TRUNK #2. WHEEL #3. ENGINE
#4. FENDER #5. BUMPER #6. HUBCAP
#7. BATTERY #8. RADIATOR

```
A V B C D T L F Q I N M R E R O
W Y P N E E G X E Z B C R U T H
D H U R N A E F N H J V E T U
Y R E I R P G J R E D T P K N B
P O G E U O N P O E F E N P M C
G N H O L T T P E R P U R G T A
E R A D I A T O R R T R O P P
P B U M P E R F Y T N U P P O J
F U E N T E U B A T T E R Y G Y
```

44. **Jumbles:** #1. RUGBY #2. ERROR #3. COACH
#4. SKIING #5. HELMET #6. FAIRWAY
Mystery Answer: UNIFORM

45. **Jumbles:** #1. OBOE #2. DRUMS #3. VIOLIN
#4. GUITAR #5. BAGPIPES #6. TROMBONE
Mystery Answer: BASSOON

46. **Jumbles:** #1. HEED—NEGLECT
#2. MORON—GENIUS #3. PEACE—WARTIME
#4. BARREN—FERTILE #5. CLUMSY—SKILLFUL
Mystery Answer: GIANT-DWARF

47. **Jumbles:** #1. FILLY #2. TRACK #3. STEED
#4. SADDLE #5. JOCKEY #6. BRONCO
#7. HARNESS #8. MUSTANG

```
R X Z F O U M Z X H J P U I C L
S Y D F Y N H U P G U O P Z S P
S A P T H F L E S O N F C E T P
E T P O R U O Y O T U U K E J
N T I U L A L P P S A D D L E K
R D P G E L C J O J O N K D Y
A Y X R I L B K L B X T G L P O
H U K F U Z W I V H T S Y C L Z
L Z U R Y T U X B R O N C O H O
```

48. **Jumbles:** #1. PITCH #2. COACH #3. SINGLE
#4. LEAGUE #5. DOUBLE #6. PLAYOFF
Mystery Answer: SCHEDULE

49. **Jumbles:** #1. TOILET #2. HURRAH #3. LITERAL
#4. CLASSIC #5. TORMENT #6. MAXIMUM
Mystery Answer: MECHANISM

50. **Jumbles:** #1. RIVER #2. BEACH #3. SWAMP
#4. TRENCH #5. GROUND #6. VOLCANO
Mystery Answer: MOUNTAIN

51. **Jumbles:** #1. FIGHT #2. TRIPLE #3. INNING
#4. TENNIS #5. HOCKEY #6. FUMBLE
Mystery Answer: OFFENSE

52. **Jumbles:** #1. TARGET #2. CANNON #3. HELMET
#4. SAMURAI #5. CAPTAIN #6. WARFARE
Mystery Answer: CAMOUFLAGE

53. **Jumbles:** #1. HOAX—TRICK
#2. VERIFY—CONFIRM #3. SHIELD—PROTECT
#4. SAVAGE—VICIOUS #5. BLAZING—BURNING
Mystery Answer: MIX—BLEND

54. **Jumbles:** #1A. OBVIOUS #5A. VULGAR
#7A. ORBIT #8A. STEEPLE #10A. GANG
#12A. FOREIGN #13A. POISON #1D. OBLONG
#2D. INNING #3D. SIGHT #4D. FLAIL #5D. VALET
#6D. REUNION #8D. SUMMON #9D. ESKIMO
#11D. ADOPT

55. **Jumbles:** #1. AVENUE #2. AUGUST #3. SUNDAY
#4. NUMBER #5. EVENING #6. FEBRUARY
Mystery Answer: DIAMETER

56. **Jumbles:** #1. ADIEU #2. AMIGO #3. INDIGO #4. INVADE #5. OPERATE #6. OBSCURE
Mystery Answer: IMPROVISE

57. **Jumbles:** #1. FINCH #2. GOOSE #3. TURKEY #4. THRUSH #5. CANARY #6. MALLARD
Mystery Answer: STARLING

58. **Jumbles:** #1. JUMPY #2. KETTLE #3. MUSTER #4. SPANISH #5. VENTURE #6. ROYALTY #7. BROTHER
Mystery Answer: SPRINKLE

59. **Jumbles:** #1. A BOTTLE #2. MONEY #3. A TREE #4. COLUMBUS #5. ZEBRA #6. SWORDFISH

60. **Jumbles:** #1. RHINO #2. CHIMP #3. LEMUR #4. TURKEY #5. GOPHER #6. CHEETAH
Mystery Answer: PORCUPINE

61. **Jumbles:** #1. IACOCCA #2. SHATNER #3. ROONEY #4. FLEMING #5. JORDAN #6. COSBY #7. CHENEY #8. NICKLAUS #9. SAWYER #10. WILLIAMS

62. **Jumbles:** #1. HONEY #2. POTATO #3. BANANA #4. TOMATO #5. BISCUIT #6. CRACKER #7. POULTRY
Mystery Answer: CHOCOLATE

63. **Jumbles:** #1. NIECE #2. UNCLE #3. HUBBY #4. FATHER #5. COUSIN #6. HUSBAND #7. DAUGHTER #8. GRANDSON

```
P F U I O H R D A U G H T E R U
U R E T Y U U R F V H N K O L P
T F E T C D B N G O P T U P N
H U N J K E U P B S P O R I O N
K G P E L T R U D Y V E P O M I
N U T C O J H N T U H P J L P S
G R N E R E A Y U T U P U L P U
R U L I F R R K A L Y L J B O O
F Y T N G C T F H U S B A N D C
```

64. **Jumbles:** #1. RUSTY #2. KNOWN #3. HORRID #4. ORNERY #5. EXTINCT #6. LOVABLE #7. BUOYANT
Mystery Answer: OBNOXIOUS

65. **Jumbles:** #1. BEE #2. SLUR #3. FINAL #4. FINISH #5. ROUTINE #6. KINDLING #7. MESSENGER #8. PHENOMENON #9. EMBARRASSED
Mystery Answer: DISAGREEABLE

66. **Jumbles:** #1. HELENA #2. JUNEAU #3. RALEIGH #4. JACKSON #5. BISMARCK #6. COLUMBUS
Mystery Answer: LANSING

67. **Jumbles:** #1. HARP #2. HORN #3. CHORD #4. MELODY #5. TRUMPET #6. HARMONY
Mystery Answer: RHYTHM

68. **Jumbles:** #1. FOUL #2. GUARD #3. BASKET #4. DRIBBLE #5. OFFENSE #6. UNIFORM
Mystery Answer: REFEREE

69. **Jumbles:** #1. FLEECE #2. VEGETABLES #3. A GLADIOLA #4. A PORCUPINE #5. THE SUN #6. A LOCUST

70. **Jumbles:** #1A. NOURISH #5A. FURROW #7A. RUMOR #8A. FORSAKE #10A. WOVE #12A. SPECIAL #13A. EXODUS #1D. NARROW #2D. REPOSE #3D. HELLO #4D. WRECK #5D. FLUSH #6D. WISHFUL #8D. FUNGUS #9D. EQUITY #11D. ORDER

71. **Jumbles:** #1. CAN #2. FILM #3. LOBBY #4. POLISH #5. ASHAMED #6. DIPLOMAT #7. DISPLEASE #8. MIRACULOUS #9. PESSIMISTIC
Mystery Answer: ACCOMPLISHED

72. **Jumbles:** #1. A SUNFISH #2. GROUND BEEF #3. I AM BUSHED #4. A CANNIBAL #5. A HAMMER #6. A PENNY

73. **Jumbles:** #1. EASILY #2. FREELY #3. WHOLLY #4. SLOWLY #5. HAPPILY #6. GINGERLY
Mystery Answer: WILLINGLY

74. **Jumbles:** #1. FUNNY #2. WEARY #3. LIVELY #4. BORING #5. ADORED #6. DEVOUT #7. JOYOUS
Mystery Answer: WONDERFUL

75. **Jumbles:** #1. MITT #2. CATCH #3. STRIKE #4. JERSEY #5. HUDDLE #6. PITCHER
Mystery Answer: STADIUM
Trivia Quiz: PITTSBURGH

76. **Jumbles:** #1. MINGLE #2. METHOD #3. MOMENT #4. MACHINE #5. MAILBOX #6. MORNING #7. MEASURE #8. MANAGER
Mystery Answer: MAGNOLIA

77. **Jumbles:** #1. PANDA #2. SLOTH #3. FERRET #4. JAGUAR #5. COYOTE #6. WEASEL #7. LEMMING
Mystery Answer: ELEPHANT

78. **Jumbles:** #1. FIVExTWO=TEN #2. SEVEN+TWO=NINE #3. FOUR-FOUR=ZERO #4. FIFTY+TEN=SIXTY
Mystery Equation: TEN x FIVE = FIFTY

79. **Jumbles:** #1. BOONE #2. EDWARDS #3. CLINTON #4. SARANDON #5. CLEMENS #6. WINSLET #7. REASONER #8. GRETZKY #9. HARVEY #10. SELLECK

80. **Jumbles:** #1. BUTTER #2. TRENCH #3. FEATURE #4. CLATTER #5. WEALTHY #6. GLAMOUR #7. WEEDLESS
Mystery Answer: DAUGHTER

81. **Jumbles:** #1. PUN #2. PURR #3. BLOND #4. BALLOT #5. TEXTURE #6. KEEPSAKE #7. BEDSPREAD #8. METICULOUS #9. SHORTHANDED
Mystery Answer: THUNDERSTORM

82. **Jumbles:** #1A. IMPOUND #5A. WARMTH #7A. AFFIX #8A. AFFRONT #10A. DUTY #12A. COCONUT #13A. LOGJAM #1D. INLAND #2D. ODDITY #3D. DWARF #4D. FROWN #5D. WHIRL #6D. HAYLOFT #8D. ACTUAL #9D. TWINGE #11D. UNCLE

83. **Jumbles:** #1. TICKET #2. CAPTAIN #3. OCTOBER #4. FREEWAY #5. DISTRICT #6. BUILDING
Mystery Answer: DUPLICATE

84. **Jumbles:** #1. SALSA #2. POLKA #3. WALTZ #4. SAMBA #5. MAMBO #6. FOXTROT #7. FANDANGO #8. BALLROOM

```
A Z C Y G I X P R Y H L Z D D A
B S B A L L R O O M A V X H F N
N L A L O P U R Z U T O E J O H
O M K L K G L T S C B T L F X K
Z E L O S U L L U M P I G N T L
D C O F S A M B A J L Z S N R O
J B P B W H G M H T B D R O O Z
C G N C U N H K X V K G P T U F
X C I C F A N D A N G O H P G Z
```

85. **Jumbles:** #1. KING #2. MOVE #3. PIECE #4. BISHOP #5. KNIGHT #6. CAPTURE
Mystery Answer: CHECKMATE

86. **Jumbles:** #1. ABACUS #2. NERVES #3. BANANA #4. OSTRICH #5. TEASPOON
Mystery Answer: EVAPORATES

87. **Jumbles:** #1. FLORIDA #2. VERMONT #3. MICHIGAN #4. KENTUCKY #5. COLORADO #6. OKLAHOMA #7. WISCONSIN
Mystery Answer: CONNECTICUT

88. **Jumbles:** #1. SUNNY #2. FLOOD #3. SYSTEM #4. THUNDER #5. WARNING #6. MONSOON
Mystery Answer: SNOWSTORM

89. **Jumbles:** #1. GLOVE #2. TENNIS #3. ROOKIE #4. DOUBLE #5. FAIRWAY #6. DIAMOND
Mystery Answer: WRESTLING

90. **Jumbles:** #1. POT ROAST #2. LIE STILL #3. A MINISTER #4. HOGWASH #5. BRAZILIANS #6. YOUR AGE

91. **Jumbles:** #1. JAGUAR #2. OCTOPUS #3. NAGASAKI #4. HAMILTON #5. HONDURAS
Mystery Answer: JOHN ADAMS

92. **Jumbles:** #1. ICY #2. IFFY #3. WOMAN #4. DIGEST #5. ACHIEVE #6. OBSTRUCT #7. COUNTDOWN #8. ACCOMPLISH #9. MERITORIOUS
Mystery Answer: CIRCUMSTANCE

93. **Jumbles:** #1A. TOPPING #5A. JURIST #7A. KAYAK #8A. MEMENTO #10A. YULE #12A. OPINION #13A. GENIUS #1D. TURKEY #2D. PALACE #3D. GUILE #4D. ERUPT #5D. JOKER #6D. TYPHOON #8D. MORGUE #9D. OFFICE #11D. USAGE

94. **Jumbles:** #1. VAULT #2. PENNY #3. BANKER #4. CHARGE #5. DOLLAR #6. INCOME
Mystery Answer: REVENUE

95. **Jumbles:** #1. RABBIT #2. JANGLE #3. LIGHTLY #4. APPOINT #5. MOBSTER #6. FUNCTION #7. PHEASANT
Mystery Answer: HILARIOUS

96. **Jumbles:** #1. SAWYER #2. INSECTS #3. MONKEES #4. TRAVOLTA #5. BADMINTON
Mystery Answer: NOVA SCOTIA

97. **Jumbles:** #1. NEEDLE #2. WILLOW #3. BAMBOO #4. FOLIAGE #5. COCONUT #6. DOGWOOD
Mystery Answer: MAGNOLIA

98. **Jumbles:** #1. RELIC #2. ROUGH #3. ROUND #4. REVISE #5. REPEAT #6. RANDOM #7. REGULAR #8. RAINBOW
Mystery Answer: ROMANTIC

99. **Jumbles:** #1. PERCH #2. GUPPY #3. SALMON #4. HALIBUT #5. CODFISH #6. PIRANHA #7. GOLDFISH #8. MACKEREL

100. **Jumbles:** #1. LIBEL #2. HITCH #3. TYRANT #4. RENDER #5. RUNNER #6. SERIOUS
Mystery Answer: NUTRITION

101. **Jumbles:** #1. LOCKLEAR #2. DUKAKIS #3. HOWARD #4. CRONKITE #5. TANDY #6. HAMILTON #7. PACINO #8. GRAHAM #9. NEWMAN #10. BRADLEY

102. **Jumbles:** #1. HUM #2. GROW #3. HONEY #4. THRIVE #5. ATTEMPT #6. FUMIGATE #7. INVENTORY #8. FLASHLIGHT #9. PREDICAMENT
Mystery Answer: AMPHITHEATER

103. **Jumbles:** #1. FOUR/TWO=TWO #2. SIX/TWO=THREE #3. NINE-ONE=EIGHT #4. ONE+SEVEN=EIGHT
Mystery Equation: EIGHT / TWO = FOUR

104. **Jumbles:** #1. LION #2. TIGER #3. HYENA #4. JACKAL #5. BADGER #6. LEOPARD
Mystery Answer: POLAR BEAR

105. **Jumbles:** #1A. LETTUCE #5A. BLIGHT #7A. AMUCK #8A. ALMANAC #10A. DUMP #12A. GLIMPSE #13A. EDGING #1D. LIZARD #2D. TEACUP #3D. EXCEL #4D. VILLA #5D. BRIAR #6D. TRAPEZE #8D. ANYONE #9D. COUPLE #11D. UTTER

106. **Jumbles:** #1. TEMPO—CADENCE #2. PRIZED—VALUED #3. SHRINK—DWINDLE #4. THWART—PREVENT #5. LAUNCH—BLASTOFF
Mystery Answer: FRANK—CANDID

107. **Jumbles:** #1. HIPPO #2. SLOTH #3. LLAMA #4. WALRUS #5. GIRAFFE #6. MUSKRAT
Mystery Answer: MARMOSET

108. **Jumbles:** #1. RECESS #2. ENROLL #3. JUNIOR #4. DEGREE #5. CAMPUS #6. SCHOLAR #7. ACADEMY #8. GRADUATE

109. **Jumbles:** #1. EAGLE #2. STORK #3. PENGUIN #4. BUZZARD #5. PEACOCK #6. SPARROW
Mystery Answer: WOODPECKER

110. **Jumbles:** #1. MUSKET #2. MISSION #3. ADMIRAL #4. WARSHIP #5. INVASION #6. GARRISON
Mystery Answer: VIETNAM WAR

111. **Jumbles:** #1. ABYSS #2. GULCH #3. GLOBE #4. GRASS #5. CLIMATE #6. PLATEAU
Mystery Answer: ATMOSPHERE

112. **Jumbles:** #1. OPERA #2. UTOPIA #3. AGENDA #4. IMPULSE #5. UPGRADE #6. ADHESIVE
Mystery Answer: ADVANTAGE

113. **Jumbles:** #1. PIANO #2. POLKA #3. OPERA #4. CHORD #5. GUITAR #6. CONCERT
Mystery Answer: PICCOLO

114. **Jumbles:** #1. JUNGLE #2. MELLOW #3. CRITTER
#4. VARNISH #5. GIZZARD #6. CUSTARD
#7. VAULTED
Mystery Answer: REDUNDANT

115. **Jumbles:** #1. DULL—BRIGHT
#2. HUSKY—SCRAWNY #3. EXPERT—NOVICE
#4. EXPIRE—CONTINUE #5. RELEASE—CAPTURE
Mystery Answer: BALD—HAIRY

116. **Jumbles:** #1. STORY #2. PROOF #3. VERIFY
#4. BYLINE #5. ANCHOR #6. HEADLINE
#7. REPORTER #8. NEWSCAST

```
V H E A D L I N E Z A R T Y O X
A B O Y Y O T T I E U E O R T Z
O R Z D D S S H P Y I T Z O I S
X Y K U D A D E O U P R I T R Y
R C D X C A N C H O R O X S P F
Z I F S I D T G A L P E O A I
F T W E L P H Z R Y P E J Y P R
D E D Y U X G F S F R R Z O O E
N A B H N I P R O O F D C D R V
```

117. **Jumbles:** #1. RETALIATE #2. HUMILIATE
#3. AGREEABLE #4. ESCALATOR #5. HARMONIZE
#6. ABANDONED
Mystery Answer: GIBRALTAR

118. **Jumbles:** #1. ORBIT #2. COMET #3. PLANET
#4. SATURN #5. URANUS #6. ECLIPSE
#7. NEPTUNE #8. MERCURY
Mystery Answer: METEORITE

119. **Jumbles:** #1. GIANTS #2. ROYALS #3. INDIANS
#4. ROCKIES #5. YANKEES #6. DODGERS
Mystery Answer: CARDINALS

120. **Jumbles:** #1. COUSIN #2. BODINE #3. MANSION
#4. WIDOWER #5. NEIGHBOR #6. DRYSDALE
Mystery Answer: BUDDY EBSEN

121. **Jumbles:** #1. MARTIN #2. COSTNER
#3. BERMUDA #4. MALAYSIA #5. MAGELLAN
Mystery Answer: CAMBODIAN

122. **Jumbles:** #1A. FLUTTER #5A. WEALTH
#7A. NEEDY #8A. HEMLINE #10A. YOGA
#12A. SKILLET #13A. NEPHEW #1D. FRENZY
#2D. TUNDRA #3D. REVUE #4D. WAKEN
#5D. WORLD #6D. HATCHET #8D. HEAVEN
#9D. EMPLOY #11D. OZONE

123. **Jumbles:** #1. MOONBEAMS #2. PENMANSHIP
#3. WISECRACKS #4. A PEDIGREE
#5. POST OFFICE #6. IGNORANT

124. **Jumbles:** #1. RIGID #2. DIRTY #3. PUSHY
#4. TRICKY #5. FEEBLE #6. DEVIOUS
#7. HIDEOUS
Mystery Answer: RIDICULOUS

125. **Jumbles:** #1A. JAVELIN #5A. VELVET #7A. KNOLL
#8A. DYNAMIC #10A. THUD #12A. EPISODE
#13A. REVERT #1D. JUNKET #2D. EYELID #3D.
NATTY #4D. ALIBI #5D. VITAL #6D. TREMBLE
#8D. DIVERT #9D. CHROME #11D. HAIRY

126. **Jumbles:** #1. BAIT #2. WORM #3. RIVER
#4. WATER #5. PERMIT #6. BOBBER #7. MINNOW
Mystery Answer: ROWBOAT

127. **Jumbles:** #1. METEOR #2. BERMUDA
#3. CHINESE #4. FLOWERS #5. PAKISTAN
Mystery Answer: PETROLEUM

128. **Jumbles:** #1. PARTY #2. FLOOR #3. HOUSE
#4. SENATE #5. ELECTED #6. SPEAKER
#7. MINORITY #8. MAJORITY

```
H S P E A K E R U I P T O P R P
Y K P R C S R M A J O R I T Y U
T R V N K R E L R O S H Y H D O
I G R U O N H O U S E F R U E P
R H R B V R O U O J N N L T T O
O H Y U L T J B V A X R Y C L
N H J I F B H K E T T U H D E U
I P U P A R T Y T W E R R O L I
M U N R U U P U T P G H K P E P
```

129. **Jumbles:** #1. HOMER #2. GOALIE #3. DEFEAT
I#4. SEASON #5. VICTORY #6. MANAGER
Mystery Answer: SCRIMMAGE

130. **Jumbles:** #1. PIERRE #2. TOPEKA #3. BOSTON
#4. OLYMPIA #5. CONCORD #6. HONOLULU
Mystery Answer: ANNAPOLIS

131. **Jumbles:** #1. OUTFIT #2. BLOUSE #3. SHORTS
#4. NECKTIE #5. APPAREL #6. PAJAMAS
#7. SWEATER #8. OVERALLS
Mystery Answer: SHOELACES

132. **Jumbles:** #1. TOPAZ #2. AMBER #3. PYRITE
#4. ZIRCON #5. QUARTZ #6. CRYSTAL
#7. EMERALD #8. DIAMOND

```
O F H G H J K U P U L H P L L K
C H B R D I A M O N D O N E O L
R U T U I L N O L B T U J N P D
Y P O J U K F V U E P Z L O N L
S H P U N G E E T Y T P F K L A
T P A M B E R I F R R I C T O R
A N Z O I O R T A R P H O P B E
L R U P U Y H U I U N Y P P H M
F U I R P U Q P Z I R C O N I E
```

133. **Jumbles:** #1. BENCH #2. GLOVE #3. OFFENSE
#4. AVERAGE #5. POSITION #6. OUTFIELD
Mystery Answer: DIVISION
Trivia Quick Quiz: RED BARBER

134. **Jumbles:** #1A. CONTROL #5A. LOCKET
#7A. WEIGH #8A. PACKAGE #10A. BOUT
#12A. FACULTY #13A. EMBRYO #1D. COBWEB
#2D. TAUGHT #D. LLAMA #4D. ICING #5D. LUCKY
#6D. TERRIFY #8D. PAPAYA #9D. EMPLOY
#11D. ORDER

135. **Jumbles:** #1. CHUMMY #2. SCRIBBLE
#3. RATIONAL #4. BANISTER #5. TRACTION
#6. MARRIAGE #7. FORMERLY
Mystery Answer: BLAMELESS

136. **Jumbles:** #1. WIN #2. PICK #3. EMPTY
#4. FACING #5. BIFOCAL #6. VELOCITY
#7. NOSEBLEED #8. RETROSPECT
#9. COMMUNICATE
Mystery Answer: COMPENSATION

137. **Jumbles:** #1. ERMINE #2. MONACO #3. JOHNSON
#4. WILLIAMS #5. NORTHWEST
Mystery Answer: CHRISTMAS

138. **Jumbles:** #1. SUGAR #2. RAVIOLI #3. PRETZEL
#4. CUSTARD #5. GOULASH #6. SEAFOOD
#7. OATMEAL
Mystery Answer: SPAGHETTI

139. **Jumbles:** #1. RIVER #2. ENSUE #3. RAZOR
#4. YEARLY #5. TALLEST #6. TONIGHT
Mystery Answer: NOTATION

140. **Jumbles:** #1. DRUMS #2. VIOLIN #3. FINALE
#4. LEGATO #5. RHYTHM #6. CANTATA
Mystery Answer: SONATA

141. **Jumbles:** #1. HUNTER #2. FRAMPTON
#3. GEPHARDT #4. BASINGER #5. COURIC
#6. POLLACK #7. BROTHERS #8. DOUGLAS
#9. BROKAW #10. BOWIE

142. **Jumbles:** #1. DAMP #2. RADAR #3. CHILLY
#4. ISOBAR #5. TWISTER #6. CYCLONE
#7. TYPHOON
Mystery Answer: PRECIPITATION

143. **Jumbles:** #1A. DISPUTE #5A. SCHEME #7A. IRISH
#8A. PETUNIA #10A. GRIM #12A. MILEAGE
#13A. OBJECT #1D. DURING #2D. POSSUM
#3D. EERIE #4D. KHAKI #5D. SIOUX
#6D. EMBRACE #8D. POLICY #9D. ATTACK
#11D. RIGOR

144. **Jumbles:** #1. DELIBERATE #2. VEGETATION
#3. FRAUDULENT #4. EXPERIMENT
#5. HORRENDOUS #6. MEMORANDUM
Mystery Answer: BANGLADESH

145. **Jumbles:** #1. RHUBARB #2. REDWOOD
#3. FLORIDA #4. SABOTAGE #5. ELEPHANT
Mystery Answer: GERALD FORD

146. **Jumbles:** #1. FRY #2. ZEST #3. TRICK
#4. RARELY #5. WEDDING #6. OVERRULE
#7. AMUSEMENT #8. GOVERNMENT
#9. NEGOTIATION
Mystery Answer: IDIOSYNCRASY

147. **Jumbles:** #1A. BILLION #5A. BEHAVE #7A. ROGUE
#8A. HEXAGON #10A. WILY #12A. OVERSEE #13A.
OCCULT #1D. BORROW #2D. LUXURY
#3D. NIECE #4D. RHINO #5D. BORAX
#6D. ENCLOSE #8D. HECKLE #9D. NAUSEA
#11D. IDIOT

148. **Jumbles:** #1. RATIO #2. NUMBER #3. ALGEBRA
#4. FORMULA #5. INFINITY #6. POSITIVE
Mystery Answer: GEOMETRY

149. **Jumbles:** #1. SUGAR #2. ALOHA #3. PACIFIC
#4. SURFING #5. BEACHES #6. VOLCANO
#7. TROPICAL #8. PINEAPPLE
Mystery Answer: PEARL HARBOR

150. **Jumbles:** #1A. ZEALOUS #5A. THATCH
#7A. LUNGE #8A. ISTHMUS #10A. TYPE
#12A. CHINOOK #13A. CHUMMY #1D. ZEALOT
#2D. LEAGUE #3D. SWISS #4D. BAYOU
#5D. TIGHT #6D. HAMMOCK #8D. INCOME
#9D. SMOOTH #11D. YUCCA

151. **Jumbles:** #1. VOCAL #2. FIDDLE #3. PEDDLE
#4. SORORITY #5. THROTTLE #6. GROUNDER
#7. BASEMENT
Mystery Answer: GERMINATE

152. **Jumbles:** #1. INTELLIGENT #2. BENEFICIARY
#3. UNORGANIZED #4. LOUDSPEAKER
#5. COMPTROLLER #6. ACKNOWLEDGE
Mystery Answer: SWITZERLAND

153. **Jumbles:** #1A. INVALID #5A. AUTUMN #7A. ATLAS
#8A. ORDERLY #10A. DUSK #12A. MOLLUSK
#13A. EGGNOG #1D. INLAND #2D. ATTACK
#3D. DONOR #4D. STALL #5D. ALLEY
#6D. NETWORK #8D. ORATOR #9D. YOGURT
#11D. UPPER

154. **Jumbles:** #1. NOISY #2. BURLY #3. BRIGHT
#4. JAGGED #5. SPECIAL #6. VICIOUS
#7. JEALOUS
Mystery Answer: UNBELIEVABLE

155. **Jumbles:** #1. LAX #2. NAVY #3. GROUP
#4. SENTRY #5. BARRIER #6. SWIMMING
#7. ASSISTANT #8. ATTACHMENT #9. RATIONALIZE
Mystery Answer: PRESERVATION

156. **Jumbles:** #1. MADAM #2. HEARTH #3. THICKET
#4. SUCCESS #5. REGULAR #6. DIAMOND
Mystery Answer: DETERMINED

157. **Jumbles:** #1A. KILLJOY #5A. VOODOO
#7A. TWEED #8A. LONGING #10A. ENVY
#12A. UTENSIL #13A. TYPIST #1D. KETTLE
#2D. LONELY #3D. YAHOO #4D. TOXIN
#5D. VERGE #6D. OATMEAL #8D. LAVISH
#9D. GLOSSY #11D. NUTTY

158. **Jumbles:** #1. MUDDLE #2. CRACKER
#3. WEDLOCK #4. SCRIBBLE #5. FLOURISH
#6. WIRELESS #7. REMEMBER
Mystery Answer: CHEERFUL

159. **Jumbles:** #1. MOW #2. NEXT #3. PUSHY
#4. BRANCH #5. BALCONY #6. BEHAVIOR
#7. APPREHEND #8. STRENGTHEN
#9. ENVIRONMENT
Mystery Answer: THOROUGHBRED

160. **Jumbles:** #1. SYMBOL—EMBLEM
#2. HERMIT—RECLUSE #3. DEDUCT—SUBTRACT
#4. PILLAGE—PLUNDER #5. FERVENT—ZEALOUS
Mystery Answer: BOTCH—FUMBLE

161. **Jumbles:** #1A. KINGDOM #5A. PEPPER
#7A. OCCUR #8A. HEROINE #10A. HAND
#12A. PUBLISH #13A. REVOLT #1D. KIBOSH
#2D. GROUND #3D. MOVIE #4D. APRON
#5D. PIVOT #6D. RUBBISH #8D. HUDDLE
#9D. EXPIRE #11D. AZURE

162. **Jumbles:** #1. LIBYA #2. KENYA #3. LIBERIA
#4. NIGERIA #5. SENEGAL #6. MOROCCO
Mystery Answer: SOMALIA

163. **Jumbles:** #1. SIZABLE #2. MASSIVE #3. IMMENSE
#4. COLOSSAL #5. GIGANTIC #6. SPACIOUS
#7. IMPOSING #8. ENORMOUS

```
G H R D C G S P A C I O U S L E
N F K C E J I O T V P E K M N
I Z J T B M A G C B N H O N A O
S Y U O U S R D A S E A N B S R
O T P H S N P N L N L O P O S M
P A B O A E O P F O T R W H I O
M T L H P T U T P F U I M V U
J O S I Z A B L E D E N C O E S
C F D E T I M M E N S E K L P R
```

164. **Jumbles:** #1. JET #2. CUTE #3. TOXIC
#4. RUNNER #5. ATTRACT #6. COLOSSAL
#7. FACSIMILE #8. MEMBERSHIP
#9. ARCHIPELAGO
Mystery Answer: BUTTERSCOTCH

165. **Jumbles:** #1. JURISDICTION #2. ABBREVIATION
#3. SATISFACTORY #4. RESPECTIVELY
#5. ARCHITECTURE #6. CONFIRMATION
Mystery Answer: INDIANAPOLIS

166. **Jumbles:** #1. JUMBLE #2. ZEALOUS #3. CRUMBLE
#4. BRITCHES #5. FOUNTAIN #6. SEEDLESS
#7. GRACIOUS
Mystery Answer: CAUTIOUS

167. **Jumbles:** #1. MONTH #2. DECADE #3. SEASON
#4. SECOND #5. MOMENT #6. INSTANT
#7. CENTURY #8. LIFETIME

168. **Tumble Words:** #1. HOWIE LONG
#2. LONG BEACH #3. BEACH TOWEL
#4. TOWEL OFF #5. OFF CENTER
#6. CENTER COURT #7. COURT ROOM
#8. ROOM KEY #9. KEY CHAIN
#10. CHAIN LETTER

169. **Tumble Words:** #1. AT LAST #2. LAST NAME
#3. NAME THAT #4. THAT GIRL #5. GIRL SCOUT
#6. SCOUT TROOP #7. TROOP LEADER
#8. LEADER BOARD #9. BOARD GAME
#10. GAME FACE

170. **Tumble Words:** #1. DR. NO #2. NO GOOD
#3. GOOD MOVIE #4. MOVIE TIMES
#5. TIMES SQUARE #6. SQUARE ONE
#7. ONE-WAY #8. WAY TICKET #9. TICKET OFFICE
#10. OFFICE SUPPLIES

171. **Tumble Words:** #1. SOCIAL SECURITY
#2. SECURITY PRISON #3. PRISON BREAK
#4. BREAK THE #5. THE LOST #6. LOST WORLD
#7. WORLD WAR #8. WAR ZONE #9. ZONE
DEFENSE #10. DEFENSE MECHANISM

172. **Tumble Words:** #1. LOOK-SEE #2. SEE RED
#3. RED CROSS #4. CROSS FIRE #4. FIRE TRUCK
#5. TRUCK STOP #6. STOP SIGN
#7. SIGN LANGUAGE #8. LANGUAGE BARRIER
#10. BARRIER REEF

173. **Tumble Words:** #1. TALK SHOW
#2. SHOW BUSINESS #3. BUSINESS NEWS
#4. NEWS FLASH #5. FLASH FLOOD
#6. FLOOD WARNING #7. WARNING SIGN
#8. SIGN OFF #9. OFF KEY #10. KEY WEST

174 **Tumble Words:** THE BAD #2. BAD BREAK
#3. BREAK THE #4. THE WEATHER
#5. WEATHER REPORT #6. REPORT CARD
#7. CARD TRICK #8. TRICK PONY #9. PONY RIDE
#10. RIDE HOME

175. **Tumble Words:** #1. ALMOST PERFECT
#2. *PERFECT STORM* #3. STORM WARNING
#4. WARNING SIGN #5. SIGN OFF #6. OFF GUARD
#7. GUARD DOG #8. DOG HOUSE
#9. HOUSE GUEST #10. GUEST QUARTERS

176. **Tumble Words:** #1. PRIVATE CLUB #2. CLUB SODA
#3. SODA POP #4. POP TEST #5. TEST OF #6. OF
LIVING #7. LIVING WILL #8. WILL POWER #9.
POWER STEERING #10. STEERING WHEEL